DISCOVER JESUS

12 Week Introductory Course
Leader's Guide

discoverjesus.today

Discover Jesus Leader's Guide
A 12 Week Introduction Course by Geoff Woodcock

Copyright © 2016 Geoff Woodcock. Freely receive, freely give. Permission is given to reproduce, distribute, store and share this material for non-commercial purposes.

Unless otherwise indicated, all Scripture quotations are from The Holy Bible, English Standard Version™ (ESV). Copyright ©2001 by Crossway Bibles, a division of Good News Publishers. Used by permission. All rights reserved.

The Discover Jesus Leader's Guide and Workbook are both available on our website for downloading and printing. If you would like to view more resources, start a Discover Jesus group, or connect with our team, please visit our website or email us:

Web | www.discoverjesus.today
Email | info@discoverjesus.today

ISBN 978-0-9941333-0-4
Version 1 (February 2016)
Published by Acacia.Media
Printed in the USA. US English spellings used.

Contents

Discover Jesus Vision v
Teaching Outline vi
Group Principles vii
Group Mechanics viii
Quick Tips for Leaders ix

1 | Creator God 1
    In the Beginning 1
    God of the Heavens 3

2 | Jesus 9
    Jesus' Birth Foretold 9
    Jesus: The Light of Revelation 11
    Revealing God 12

3 | The Father of Love 21
    The Father's Heart 21
    The Younger Son 23
    The Elder Son 26

4 | Jesus and the Father 35
    Father + Son = 1 36
    Son of God 38
    God the Word with God 38
    Only God with God 40

5 | Jesus the Reality 45
    One Way 45
    Word of Reality 47
    Spirit of Reality 48
    Imagining the Impossible 50

6 | Image of God 55
    Created in His Image 56
    An Image Lost 58

7 | Paying the Debt 67
    Sin as a Weighty Debt 69
    Life-Debt Nailed 71
    Forgiving the Debt 72

8 | The Cross 79
    Justified 81
    Not Guilty 82
    Prophecy of the Lamb 85

9 | Resurrection Life 93
    Immersed into Death and Life 97
    The Old Self 99

10 | Grace through Faith 105
    Baptism 107
    Forgiveness through the Blood 108
    Removing Sin 109
    By Grace, Through Faith 111
    Faith of the Heart 112

11 | Born Again 119
    Born Again 119
    The Image of God 121

12 | A New Beginning 129
    Eternal Life 129
    The Only Way 130
    Counting the Cost 131
    Day of Salvation 134
    Where to from Here? 137

Discover Jesus Vision

The vision behind the *Discover Jesus* course is to create disciples: true believers who are fully devoted to following and loving Jesus. We do this in two ways:
1. by actively sharing the love of God
2. by teaching a biblical view of who God is and what it means to follow Jesus.

The teaching starts out by focusing people on asking why God created us. God designed us with a clear purpose and we cannot define that purpose for ourselves. We can only discover our purpose from God Himself. And He only shows us His design through Jesus.

In the studies we look at the different ways that Jesus reveals the Father and who He created us to be. We discover that we were created through Jesus and *for Him.* We look at how Jesus died and rose again to free us from our selfishness and sin and to restore us into His image. We look at the awesome wonder of living in the image of God, but also at the cost of following Jesus. If we are to be His disciples we must take up our cross and let Him redefine our lives so that we can live in unity and love with Jesus.

Our goal is not just to help people to understand the gospel, but to entice people to enter into a romance with Jesus. We are preparing people to love Jesus with all their hearts. Those who make a decision to follow Jesus at the end of the course will be people who are willing to live fully *for Jesus* by devoting their lives to loving God and others.

The Bible study series spans 12 weeks, depending on the group dynamics. At the end of the course, if people want to continue meeting together to study the word of God then we have more studies and resources available. These can be found online at www.discoverjesus.today.

Teaching Outline

The course content is set out in the following way:

1. God created us with a specific design and clear purpose for our lives. If we want to a sense of fulfillment in life then we need to discover God's design and purpose for us.
2. God is so awesome that we cannot discover Him by our own efforts. God must make Himself known to us. The same is true for our purpose in life—God must reveal it to us.
3. God has revealed Himself to us through Jesus.
4. Jesus shows us that God is love: infinite, awesome, absolute, unwavering, eternal, unlimited love.
5. Jesus is God.
6. Jesus is also the image of God. We were created in the image of God to live in unity with Jesus.
7. We all rejected the image of God and lived instead for ourselves. We all traded a life of love for a life of selfishness.
8. By living for self we incurred an immeasurable life-debt towards God.
9. Jesus took our debt at the cross and secured our forgiveness.
10. Jesus rose again, enabling us to be restored into His image.
11. Having taken our sin, Jesus fills us with the life of His Spirit so we can live in the reality of His image.
12. The only way to be restored into the image of God is to receive the free gift by faith. Faith is the real belief of the heart.
13. Through faith, we also receive eternal life. This is life in unity with Jesus both now and forever.
14. Following Jesus is costly. It requires us to give our entire lives to God and devote all our time, energy, and resources to loving God and loving others.

The Study Series ends with an invitation to follow Jesus.

Group Principles

"By this all people will know that you are my disciples,
if you have love for one another." John 13:35

It is by our love that people will know we are disciples of Jesus. Love is the defining quality of being a disciple, however love is not just taught—it is experienced. A genuine love within leaders is therefore an essential aspect of this course. The love of the leaders frames everything that is taught and allows people to experience what fellowship and unity is like within the Body of Christ. This means a few things:

Love Assume that everyone in the group will end up following Jesus and is worth loving and investing in now. If you become aware of a need in someone's life, do what you can to meet that need. Seek help from others if required. If you are unable to meet that need then pray.

Fellowship Show a real interest in people. Ask questions. Love by listening more than speaking. Honor others by offering decent food and drink. Enjoy the company.

Life Speak words of life. Avoid negative words. Don't criticize or embarrass anyone. See the person through God's eyes. Treat each person like you would treat Jesus.

Freedom Don't panic if someone doesn't want to make a decision to follow Jesus and don't take it personally. We're not selling a product on commission so let people be free to choose without fear or compulsion. Remember that God won't give up on them and it might not be the right time just yet. Be kind towards those who aren't yet ready.

Grace Our goal is to entice people to enter into a romance with Jesus. We are preparing them for love. So have grace. Let people be who they are without trying to fix their lives or make them holy right away. Orientate people towards love before righteousness so that they know that transformation comes from the inside out. As God changes people's hearts, their outward behavior will naturally change as well.

Group Mechanics

Group Size The course is best done with groups of four to eight people. If there are more than eight people then consider splitting into two separate groups. Where possible it is useful to have two mature believers who can share the group leadership and help to create an atmosphere of love.

Location Use a location that suits small groups. Homes are ideal as they create a sense of family and facilitate love, fellowship and participation within the group.

Food Start with some great food and drink. Allow around half an hour for fellowship over food at the start. Give space for people to share. You can use the home reading as a starting point for leading conversation towards spiritual things.

Study The studies are built around Scripture readings and questions. The most effective way to teach someone the Bible is to draw knowledge out rather than put it in. When we teach material and give people the answers, those answers are ours, not theirs. However when we ask people questions, they own their answers. Drawing people out through questions shows respect and creates a sense of ownership of the truth.

Home Reading Each week there are around three passages of Scripture to read at home. There are then some questions to answer and some scenarios to imagine. Imagination engages the heart as well as the mind in the truth of God and is a great way of building faith.

There are also three chapters of John for people to read at home, a prayer to pray, and some space to write down questions and experiences. This encourages people to keep an eye out for God's love and work in their lives.

It is recommended that leaders also do the home reading each week. The group can use some of the fellowship time at the beginning of each session to share about the home reading and experiences.

Quick Tips for Leaders

Take your Time
Spend some time letting people chat and get to know each other (especially on the first night). Have some drinks and food available and take an interest in people. If you become aware of a need within the group, do what you can to meet that need.

Don't feel in a hurry to get through all the material. If you don't complete a study in a single night, you can continue it in the next session.

Understand the Big Picture
The goal of this course is not to get conversions but to inspire people to become followers and disciples of Jesus. So don't manipulate or put people under pressure to make a decision for Christ. Just be loving, encouraging and kind, and let the Holy Spirit do His job.

Read the Passage and then Recap
Have someone read the passage of Scripture and then ask someone in the group to rephrase the passage in their own words. This helps everyone to focus when listening to Scripture and to process what they are reading and hearing. If some key points are missed, open it up to the group. If no one can provide a recap then get someone in the group to read the passage again.

A brief recap has been provided in *italics*. It covers the key points to draw out in case the group miss something in their recap.

Ask the Questions
Questions are essential to learning and engaging people in the material. We want to focus on drawing understanding out more than pouring information in. It can even be useful to leave people with some unanswered questions. These can help spur people on to seeking God.

Feel free to ask your own questions during discussions to lead people deeper. Gently keep people on track if they start to wander too far off topic.

The words in *italics* after the questions are for your own ideas—you can add them into the discussion and reword or build on them as you like.

Read the Quotes

Get someone in the group to read out the paragraphs that are marked with a grey quote mark on the left side. Material in these sections will often lead into the next question. Check if people have understood what has been said or if they have any questions about it.

Provoke the Imagination
Intellectual understanding only goes a small way towards spiritual growth. Learning to engage our imagination with the truth of God helps us to see the truth with the "eyes of our heart" and get a vision for how God could transform our lives through His truth. Therefore don't be afraid to challenge the imagination on occasion. For example, when the group reads of the love of the Father, ask "can you imagine what it would be like to experience that kind of love?" Imagination lets people put themselves in the picture of Scripture.

Sum Up
At the end of each study do a quick recap to go over the main points. One is provided in the summary section, but you can just use your own words.

Pray
After a few weeks, consider making some room to pray together. Anyone can pray, regardless of whether they have made a commitment to God or not. Don't put people under any pressure to pray. Instead just encourage people to feel free and be honest with God. We don't need to get all the words right or make good sounding prayers. Just express the heart.

1 | Creator God

Leader's Notes

This study is shorter to allow people more time to get to know each other. The idea behind this study is to encourage people to know that we have all been made by a good God who values us and has a real purpose for each of us. If we are going to discover our true design and purpose in life then we need to find out from God Himself exactly why He created us.

Key Goals

- To show that we are created beings with a God-given purpose and design.
- To show that only God can reveal why He created us.
- To show that God is awesome beyond all imagination.

Remember: Get someone to read the Scriptures and someone else to recap what they've heard. Involve different people.

In the Beginning

Genesis 1:1, 26-27

[1] In the beginning, God created the heavens and the earth…[26] Then God said, "Let us make man in our image, after our likeness. And let them have dominion over the fish of the sea and over the birds of the heavens and over the livestock and over all the earth and over every creeping thing that creeps on the earth." [27] So God created man in his own image, in the image of God he created him; male and female he created them.

Recap *God created the universe and He also created us in His image.*

Q: What does it mean to be created? What is our purpose in life?
- *Just listen and draw out people's ideas about meaning and purpose in life (without correcting or teaching them).*

Q: What does the world tell us about our purpose in life?
- *World media tells us that our purpose is simply to work, play and buy stuff.*
- *In terms of human design, modern education focuses on evolution which denies a creator and in doing so denies that we have any purpose beyond survival and procreation.*
- *Is there more to life than just working/eating/sleeping/dying?*

Q: Can we make up our own purpose for our life?
- *When a person creates something, it always has a purpose beyond its own existence. And this purpose is determined by the person, not the creation.*
- *The same principle is true for us. We did not create ourselves. God designed and created us and it wasn't just for our own benefit.*
- *As our Creator, God alone has determined our purpose. We cannot make it up for ourselves. We need to seek God to reveal our reason, meaning and purpose in life.*

Psalm 139:13-14

[13] For You formed my inward parts;
   You wove me in my mother's womb.
[14] I will give thanks to You, for I am fearfully [awesomely] and wonderfully made;
   Wonderful are Your works,
   And my soul knows it very well.

Recap *God made us wonderfully well.*

Q: What does this passage tell you about the value of your life?
- *God made us awesomely well and He values us as His creation.*

As people, we were not created by chance. Not a single feature of the awesome complexity that is human life came about as a result of random changes in nature. Every part of us: body, soul and spirit has been deliberately designed and wonderfully made by God. And if we are deliberately designed by God, it is because He has a definite purpose for us. He has a reason for giving us life.

With this in mind, the goal of this course is basically to explore these questions:
1. Who is God?
2. Who are we?
3. Who did God create us to be?

God of the Heavens

Psalm 113:4-6
⁴ The LORD is high above all nations;
   His glory is above the heavens.
⁵ Who is like the LORD our God,
   Who is enthroned on high,
⁶ Who humbles Himself to behold
   The things that are in heaven and in the earth?

Recap *God is so high and glorious that He has to humble himself to look at His creation.*

Q: What does it mean for God to humble Himself?
- *God holds back His awesomeness and doesn't demand the extreme glory He deserves. It's like when we talk with young children. We don't use long words they can't understand. Instead we happily humble ourselves and choose simpler words in order to be understood.*

Q: Why does God need to humble Himself to look at the universe?
- *God is simply so awesome that even the entire universe is too small for His glory. Yet God happily humbles Himself to engage with His creation.*

> The universe is made up of countless stars and planets within countless galaxies. We can't get our minds around the billions of stars in our own galaxy, let alone imagine the incredible scale of the entire universe.
>
> We are so small and insignificant that we exalt ourselves to study the stars. Yet God is so infinitely great that He has to humble Himself just to look upon the universe that exists so far beneath Him. Why? Because God is the Creator, the universe is created. God is spiritual, the universe is material. God is eternal, the universe is temporal. God is infinite, and the universe is finite. Therefore God has to humble Himself to look at a physical universe that exists on a level so far below His eternal glory.

Q: If we cannot even comprehend the creation, how can we possibly comprehend the Creator?

- *Can we imagine a God so infinite and glorious that He has to humble Himself and hold back His glory in order to look upon His creation?*
- *How much more must God humble Himself in order to interact with us?*

Q: If we cannot comprehend God then how can we possibly come to know God?

- *There is nothing we could do to know God. The only way we can know God is if He makes Himself known to us.*

Summary

> God created us with a clearly defined purpose. However, we cannot discover God or His purposes for us by ourselves. He is too awesome for our minds to conceive. The only way we can discover who God is and why He has created us is if He makes Himself and His purposes known to us.
>
> And that is exactly what He has done. God has been working throughout history to reveal Himself and the Bible has recorded some amazing insights into the nature and purposes of God. But His ultimate purpose for humanity was kept secret until a specific time: the time of Love. At that time God would reveal Himself in a new and amazing way. He would express His love and display His nature as it had never been seen before. He would reveal what He is really like and it would change the world forever.

1| Home Reading and Questions

☐ **Isaiah 40:21-31**
Take some time one evening to look at the stars above. There are only around 2000 stars visible on a clear night with the naked eye. Using current technology, astronomers roughly estimate there are more than 70 billion trillion (7×10^{22}) stars in the universe, and countless planets.

I: Imagine a God who could create all the stars and give each and every star a name. Imagine a God who needs to humble Himself just to look at His stars. Imagine that this great God intentionally created you.

Q: How is it even possible that God would know every star *by name*?

Q: Why would God create me?

☐ **Matthew 6:25-34, Matthew 10:26-33**
Take some time to imagine a God who knows us so well that He has numbered every hair on our heads. God is a God of details. He takes time to name the stars and to count the hairs. He cares for us more than we can know or understand.

I: Imagine a God who deeply loves you and cares for you. Imagine the Creator of the Universe personally promising to look after you and give you everything you need in life.

Q: What do I really need?

Q: What would it be like to never have to worry about anything ever again?

☐ **Psalm 139**

God fills the entire earth and universe with His presence. There is nowhere we can go to escape His presence. God has always been present with us at every point in our lives, regardless of whether we knew it or not.

I: Imagine a God that knows every word and every thought before you do. Imagine a God who knew you before He created you and who is intimately aware of everything you think, say and do. Imagine a God of love, powerful enough to bring His love into every detail of your life.

Q: Has God really been with me my entire life?

Q: Why does God so much care about me?

Q: How can I receive God's love?

☐ **Prayer** God, if this is all true and you are really with me, then please show me and help me to believe. If you are real then please reveal yourself to me. If you created me then please show me why.

☐ **John 1- John 3**
Write down your questions here:

☐ Experiences with God
Write down some of your own prayers, discoveries, questions and experiences.

2 | Jesus

Leader's Notes
This study introduces Jesus. It shows us how Jesus came to reveal God to us.

Key Goals
- To show how the birth of Jesus was special and prophesied in advance.
- To show how Jesus was sent to reveal God through His teachings and life.
- To get people used to asking "what does this reveal about God" when reading the Bible.

Jesus' Birth Foretold

In the Bible, a prophet is someone who God would speak clearly to. The job of the prophet was to relay God's word to people, cities and nations. In 730BC God spoke to a prophet called Isaiah and revealed that God would send a child, who would become a king over His people forever.

Over 700 years later that child was born to a young woman named Mary in a small town called Bethlehem. Mary named the child *Jesus*. In the Bible, the books of Matthew, Mark, Luke and John (also known as the gospels or good news) tell of Jesus' life and teachings.

Isaiah 7:14
Therefore the Lord himself will give you a sign. Behold, the virgin shall conceive and bear a son, and shall call his name Immanuel [meaning *God with us*].

Matthew 1:18-23
[18] Now the birth of Jesus Christ took place in this way. When his mother Mary had been betrothed to Joseph, before they came together she was found to be with child from the Holy Spirit. [19] And her husband Joseph, being a just man and unwilling to put

her to shame, resolved to divorce her quietly. [20] But as he considered these things, behold, an angel of the Lord appeared to him in a dream, saying, "Joseph, son of David, do not fear to take Mary as your wife, for that which is conceived in her is from the Holy Spirit. [21] She will bear a son, and you shall call his name Jesus, for he will save his people from their sins." [22] All this took place to fulfill what the Lord had spoken by the prophet:

[23] "Behold, the virgin shall conceive and bear a son, and they shall call his name Immanuel" (which means, God with us).

Recap *The Holy Spirit formed Jesus within Mary. God spoke to Joseph and told him to name the child "Jesus" which means "God (Yahweh) saves".*

Q: How could Isaiah know 700 years beforehand that Jesus would be born?
- *God told Isaiah about it.*

Q: Why did God send Jesus?
- *To save us (we'll look more at this a little later on). But is that all?*

Luke 2:21-32 (NASB)
[21] And when eight days had passed, before His circumcision, His name was then called Jesus, the name given by the angel before He was conceived in the womb. [22] And when the days for their purification according to the law of Moses were completed, they brought Him up to Jerusalem to present Him to the Lord [23] (as it is written in the Law of the Lord, "every firstborn male that opens the womb shall be called holy to the Lord"), [24] and to offer a sacrifice according to what was said in the Law of the Lord, "a pair of turtledoves or two young pigeons."

[25] And there was a man in Jerusalem whose name was Simeon; and this man was righteous and devout, looking for the consolation of Israel; and the Holy Spirit was upon him. [26] And it had been revealed to him by the Holy Spirit that he would not see death before he had seen the Lord's Christ. [27] And he came in the Spirit into the temple; and when the parents brought in the child Jesus, to carry out for Him the custom of the Law, [28] then he took Him into his arms, and blessed God, and said, [29]

"Now Lord, You are releasing Your bond-servant to depart in peace, According to Your word; ³⁰ For my eyes have seen Your salvation, ³¹ which You have prepared in the presence of all peoples, ³² a light of revelation to the Gentiles, and the glory of Your people Israel."

Recap *Joseph and Mary take Jesus into the temple to dedicate Him to God with an offering. Simeon sees Jesus and blesses Him, calling Him God's salvation and a light of revelation to the Gentiles. Note: the term "Gentiles" refers to non-Jews—people who are not a part of the nation of Israel.*

Q: Why is Jesus called a light of revelation? What is He revealing?
- *He is called a light of revelation because Jesus was sent to reveal God.*

Q: Who is Jesus revealing God to?
- *Everyone.*

Jesus: The Light of Revelation

Matthew 11:25-27
²⁵ At that time Jesus declared, "I thank you, Father, Lord of heaven and earth, that you have hidden these things from the wise and understanding and revealed them to little children; ²⁶ yes, Father, for such was your gracious will. ²⁷ All things have been handed over to me by my Father, and no one knows the Son except the Father, and no one knows the Father except the Son and anyone to whom the Son chooses to reveal him.

Recap *God has revealed things to little children. We can only know the Father if Jesus reveals Him to us.*

Q: Who is the Father that Jesus is talking about?
- *The One True God, the Creator of All Things.*

Q: Why is Jesus the only one who knows the Father?
- *Just get some thoughts.*

Q: What does it mean for Jesus to reveal God to us?
- *We can get to know God and experience what He's like through Jesus.*

Q: How does Jesus reveal God to us?
- *Through His life and His teachings and our relationship with Him.*

Q: What does it mean to become like little children?
- *To set aside our agendas and ideas and come to God with simple hearts that just want to know Him.*

Q: Is there any way that we could get to know God apart from Jesus?
- *Get some thoughts.*

Revealing God

Jesus reveals the Father through His teaching and His life. In this section we'll look at some of Jesus' teachings and how they show us what God is like.

Revealing a God of Love

Matthew 22:34-40

34 But when the Pharisees heard that he had silenced the Sadducees, they gathered together. 35 And one of them, a lawyer, asked him a question to test him. 36 "Teacher, which is the great commandment in the Law?" 37 And he said to him, "You shall love the Lord your God with all your heart and with all your soul and with all your mind. 38 This is the great and first commandment. 39 And a second is like it: You shall love your neighbor as yourself. 40 On these two commandments depend all the Law and the Prophets."

Recap *Some people question Jesus about the Law. Jesus says that the greatest command is to love God with all our heart, soul and mind. The second command is to love other people like they were us.*

Q: What does Jesus' teaching here show us about God?
- *That God wants our love above everything else.*
- *That God's nature is one of love.*
- *That following the rules without love is not what God wants.*

" All the commandments of the Bible and all the prophecies depend entirely on love. That means when we read a command in Scripture, we need to interpret it through the lens of love. Without love, we have only legalism: a stressful life in which we strive in vain to keep the rules and commands of Scripture. However with love, we have the power of God's nature within us, which leads us to do good works *naturally and willingly*.

Revealing a God who Provides

Luke 12:22-31

²² And he said to his disciples, "Therefore I tell you, do not be anxious about your life, what you will eat, nor about your body, what you will put on. ²³ For life is more than food, and the body more than clothing. ²⁴ Consider the ravens: they neither sow nor reap, they have neither storehouse nor barn, and yet God feeds them. Of how much more value are you than the birds! ²⁵ And which of you by being anxious can add a single hour to his span of life? ²⁶ If then you are not able to do as small a thing as that, why are you anxious about the rest? ²⁷ Consider the lilies, how they grow: they neither toil nor spin, yet I tell you, even Solomon in all his glory was not arrayed like one of these. ²⁸ But if God so clothes the grass, which is alive in the field today, and tomorrow is thrown into the oven, how much more will he clothe you, O you of little faith! ²⁹ And do not seek what you are to eat and what you are to drink, nor be worried. ³⁰ For all the nations of the world seek after these things, and your Father knows that you need them. ³¹ Instead, seek his kingdom, and these things will be added to you.

Recap *God looks after the animals. How much more will He look after us? We don't need to worry about our basic needs in life, so long as we seek His kingdom.*

Q: What does this teaching show us about God?
- *That He is a good God and He looks after His creation.*
- *That He promises to give us everything we need in life if we follow Him.*
- *That He does not want us to be anxious about anything, but to trust Him.*

Revealing a God who Heals

Matthew 8:1-3
¹ When Jesus came down from the mountain, large crowds followed Him. ² And a leper came to Him and bowed down before Him, and said, "Lord, if You are willing, You can make me clean." ³ Jesus stretched out His hand and touched him, saying, "I am willing; be cleansed." And immediately his leprosy was cleansed.

Recap *A leper comes to Jesus and says "if you are willing..." Jesus is willing and He heals Him.*

Q: What does this passage reveal about God?
- *That He has power to heal.*
- *That He likes to heal people.*

It is interesting to note that at the time leprosy was considered to be highly contagious and so no one would touch or even go near a leper for fear of the disease. Lepers led lonely lives, isolated from people and void of physical connection. It was a physically, psychologically, socially and emotionally crushing condition. Jesus had previously healed many people just by speaking out the words. But in this case He reached out His hand and touched the untouchable. By doing so, Jesus revealed not only the power of God, but the tender love and compassion of God.

Revealing a God who Forgives (if time allows)

Luke 17:1-4
¹ And he said to his disciples, "Temptations to sin are sure to come, but woe to the one through whom they come! ² It would be better for him if a millstone were hung around his neck and he were cast into the sea than that he should cause one of these little ones to sin.
³ Pay attention to yourselves! If your brother sins, rebuke him, and if he repents, forgive him, ⁴ and if he sins against you seven times in the day, and turns to you seven times, saying, 'I repent,' you must forgive him."

Recap *It's a terrible thing to cause someone to sin. If someone does sin against us, even lots of times, then we need to always forgive them.*

Q: What does it mean to sin?
- *To sin is to act against the nature of God, by doing things that grieve Him.*

Q: What does this teaching tell us about God?
- *That God considers sin to be a serious deal.*
- *That God is relentless in forgiving us.*

Summary

In the Old Testament, God primarily revealed Himself through prophets: people He would speak to clearly who would then relay His word to the people. But then, at the perfect time, God revealed Himself in the person of Jesus Christ. The things that Jesus did, the teachings Jesus shared, and the life He led, all reveal something of the awesome nature of God to us.

To really get this revelation, we need to become like little children in our hearts. We need to lay aside our skepticism, our agendas, our biases and hang-ups, and just listen to really hear what Jesus has to say. If we can take Jesus at His word then He will not only reveal the Father to us, but He will also show us exactly why God created us.

2 | Home Reading and Questions

☐ **Matthew 9:10-13**
The Pharisees were religious leaders of the Jewish people. They were offended that Jesus would spend time with sinners—people who would regularly act against the loving nature of God. Some of these people like the tax collectors would cheat, lie and steal as a way of life. Some were prostitutes. Some were alcoholics. There were many who were hooked on the self-destructive pleasures of life. The Pharisees were worried that hanging out with such people would drag them down into sin. But Jesus saw the whole situation differently.

Q: What does this Bible passage teach me about the nature of God?

Q: Why would Jesus want to spend time with people if they were sinners?

Q: What does Jesus mean "I desire compassion, and not sacrifice"?

Q: Would Jesus want to hang out with me?

☐ **Luke 15:1-10**
The Pharisees still can't get over the fact that Jesus spends so much time with sinners. Here Jesus decides to tackle the issue head-on. He shows us that God does not write-off people who go their own way and do their own thing. Instead He seeks us out. He searches for us like a lost coin. Like a shepherd searching for a lost sheep, Jesus keeps on calling out to us until He finds us.

Q: Have I gone my own way in life?

Q: Is God really searching for me?

Q: Can I sense God calling me to come to Him?

I: Imagine being a young person whose fiancée has got lost on a hike. How hard would you search to find your true love? Or imagine being a father or mother, whose only child is lost. Would you ever give up the search for your lost child?

Now imagine God. A God who never tires, and who never gives up the search for the one He loves. Imagine a God of unfailing love, relentlessly calling out your name. Imagine yourself lost. Where are you? Are you running and trying to find your own way to safety? Have you stopped running? Or are you turning towards the sound of the voice?

☐ **Prayer** God, if you're really searching for me, can you help me to hear your call? Can you help me to know in my heart that you love me and that you'll take care of me?

☐ **John 4 - John 6**
Write down your questions here:

☐ **Experiences with God**
Write down some of your own prayers, discoveries, questions and experiences.

3 | The Father of Love

Leader's Notes
This study looks at some key aspects of the Father's nature.

Key Goals
- To show people how much God loves them.
- To inspire people to turn to God.

 In the last study we looked at some of the ways Jesus revealed the Father. In this study we are going to focus on one specific teaching in which Jesus not only reveals what God is like, but also reveals what we are like.

The Father's Heart

Luke 15:11-32
[11] And he said, "There was a man who had two sons. [12] And the younger of them said to his father, 'Father, give me the share of property that is coming to me.' And he divided his property between them. [13] Not many days later, the younger son gathered all he had and took a journey into a far country, and there he squandered his property in reckless living. [14] And when he had spent everything, a severe famine arose in that country, and he began to be in need. [15] So he went and hired himself out to one of the citizens of that country, who sent him into his fields to feed pigs. [16] And he was longing to be fed with the pods that the pigs ate, and no one gave him anything.

[17] "But when he came to himself, he said, 'How many of my father's hired servants have more than enough bread, but I perish here with hunger! [18] I will arise and go to my father, and I will say to him, "Father, I have sinned against heaven and before you. [19] I am no longer worthy to be called your son. Treat me as one of your hired servants."' [20] And he arose and came to his father. But while he was still a long way

off, his father saw him and felt compassion, and ran and embraced him and kissed him. [21] And the son said to him, 'Father, I have sinned against heaven and before you. I am no longer worthy to be called your son.' [22] But the father said to his servants, 'Bring quickly the best robe, and put it on him, and put a ring on his hand, and shoes on his feet. [23] And bring the fattened calf and kill it, and let us eat and celebrate. [24] For this my son was dead, and is alive again; he was lost, and is found.' And they began to celebrate.

[25] "Now his older son was in the field, and as he came and drew near to the house, he heard music and dancing. [26] And he called one of the servants and asked what these things meant. [27] And he said to him, 'Your brother has come, and your father has killed the fattened calf, because he has received him back safe and sound.' [28] But he was angry and refused to go in. His father came out and entreated him, [29] but he answered his father, 'Look, these many years I have served you, and I never disobeyed your command, yet you never gave me a young goat, that I might celebrate with my friends. [30] But when this son of yours came, who has devoured your property with prostitutes, you killed the fattened calf for him!' [31] And he said to him, 'Son, you are always with me, and all that is mine is yours. [32] It was fitting to celebrate and be glad, for this your brother was dead, and is alive; he was lost, and is found.'"

Recap *There were two sons. One demanded his share of the inheritance. He blew his inheritance on wild living and ended up feeding pigs in order to survive. He then came to his senses and decided to return home to see if his father would accept him back as a servant. His father accepted him back as a son, and they celebrated. The elder brother was angry about it all, and the father tried to talk him out of his anger.*

> This story is one of many parables in the Bible. A parable is a metaphor—a story loaded with symbolism that can deliver a deeper message straight to the heart. However, if we miss the symbolism then we miss the message. So we need to slow down and take some time with the story to think about what Jesus is really saying.

Q: Who is the father in the parable?
- *God.*

Q: Who are the sons?
- *At the time, the elder son represented those Jewish people who had not strayed off into wild living, but neither had they taken hold of all the blessings that God wanted to give them.*
- *The younger son represented people who were wasting their lives on the pleasures and pursuits of the world.*

Q: What does this parable reveal about God?
- *Get some ideas. Don't give any answers.*

The Younger Son

Q: What was the younger son missing out on while he lived in the far country?
- *The experience of the father's love. His provision. Relationship. Intimacy. Connection. Purpose. Blessing. Work. Family.*

Q: Why did the younger son leave in the first place?
- *The draw of the pleasures of the world? Pressure to create a life for himself?*

> When the younger son left his family behind, he also disconnected himself from his identity within the family. He went to a land where he would not be recognized, where he could be free to indulge in wasteful living. He denied who he was—his place in his family and community—all in the pursuit of pleasure.

Q: Why did he return?
- *Because of the famine. He returned because he knew that life at home was better.*

Q: Do you think he would have returned if there was no famine?
- *Often people will only turn to God in a time of crisis. If there is no crisis then people carry on living life according to their own plans, enjoying the identity they have made for themselves, never realizing how much of God's love and blessing they are missing.*

Q: What was his plan?
- *To apologize and offer himself as a servant to his father.*

Q: What does this tell us about his identity?
- *He felt that he had forfeited his identity as a son in the family and was now only barely worthy of becoming a servant in the house.*

Q: What does this mean for us?
- *If we turn to God, it's easy to feel like we're not worthy of His love and blessing when we've wasted so much of what He has given us. It's natural to want to earn our way back into relationship with him—to work for God in the hope that if we can make up for our failures by serving God well then He will accept us and bless us.*

Q: What happened when the Father saw the son coming?
- *Luke 15:20 - And he arose and came to his father. But while he was still a long way off, his father saw him and felt compassion, and ran and embraced him and kissed him.*

Q: What is Jesus telling us about God?
- *Even when we're a long way off, He is looking for us. His heart is full of compassion for us. As soon as we turn to Him, He runs to us. When all we have to offer God is the broken remains of a wasted life, He hugs us and kisses us and cries with joy over us.*

Q: Why does the Father love the son so much? Does the younger son deserve the Father's love?
- *The Father loves because it's in his nature to love. It has nothing to do with whether the younger son deserves love or not. Love is not earned by what we do. It is not a reward for being good. Love is a gift. God loves because He is love. He can't help it. He is love and He never changes, so by necessity He must always love us, even if we are going our own way and wasting our lives. He will always and at all times love us.*

Q: Did the younger son offer himself as a servant to his father as he had planned?
- *No.*

Q: Why not?
- *The father cut him off before he could say the words. Why? The father wouldn't allow the son to consider any other identity than the one that the father had given him: that of a son in the house.*

Q: What does the robe represent?
- *The father gave the son the best robe. This showed everyone that the son was fully restored into his place within the family. The father's love and acceptance and approval of the son was absolute, and it was put on display for everyone to see. It was as if the son's sinful life was completely washed away and he was transformed in a moment of inexpressible love.*

Q: What does the ring represent?
- *In ancient times, a ring was a sign of authority, belonging and identity. That ring was given to the son to show everyone that he was an empowered member of the family and that the full authority and protection of the father was given to the son.*

Q: What do the sandals represent?
- *In ancient times, free people wore sandals and slaves were forced to go barefoot. The parable implies that when the son "hired himself out" to one of the citizens of the land, he effectively became a slave and his sandals were taken away.*
- *By giving sandals to the son, the father confirmed that he would not accept the son as a slave or servant, but only as a son.*

Q: What did they do to celebrate?
- *Had a big celebration with the best food, music and dancing.*

Q: So what does all this tell us about God?
- *That God loves us beyond what we can imagine. It shows us that we don't deserve His love, but that God loves us regardless of what we've done with our lives so far or how far we have wandered from home. He continually looks for us and offers us His love as a free gift. Even though we may feel like we need to do something to earn His love or affection; even though we may think we could never be more than a servant to God, He refuses to let us settle for anything less than being a child back in the arms of our Father. God wants the best for us, better than we could imagine. All we need to do is turn to God and He will accept us and bless us beyond what we could hope or ask for. When we return to God, He celebrates and rejoices, and invites us to join in the party.*

The Elder Son

The story that Jesus told is about the father's love for both of his sons. The elder son is quite different from his brother. He didn't leave home. He didn't waste his life pursuing pleasure. He worked hard to please his father at home. But with the return of the younger son and the celebrations that began, an underlying anger rose up within the elder son.

Q: Why did the elder son get angry?
- *Because it didn't seem fair. He had served His father for years without celebration or small reward. It just wasn't fair.*

Q: What was the father's response?
- *He said that he was always with him, and that everything the father had was his.*

Q: If everything that the father had was shared with the elder son then what was the problem? Why didn't the elder son take a young goat to enjoy with his friends?
- *Because he didn't know that everything the father had was already given to him.*
- *He was waiting for the father to reward him for all his acts of service and obedience.*

> The elder son represents those people who have made their personal religion one of "doing the right things" (and "not doing the wrong things"). Deep down the elder son believed that the affection and approval of his father needed to be earned through obedience. So he called his father to look at how much he had done for him: "Look, these many years I have served you, and I never disobeyed your command, yet you never gave me a young goat, that I might celebrate with my friends". The son believed that he had done enough to earn his father's blessing, whereas the younger son had done nothing at all to earn it. So it didn't seem fair when the father lavished the younger son with love, affection and approval. That kind of love seemed offensive.

Q: Did the father love the elder son any less than the younger?
- *No. He had already given everything he had to the elder son.*

Q: So why did the elder son not enjoy the riches that were his?
- *Because he thought that he had to earn them first.*

Q: What does this show us about ourselves?
- *Thinking that we need to earn love is a hard mindset to break.*

Q: Is it possible to go our own way in life, but still enjoy the Father's love and blessing?
- *Going our own way in life causes us to waste and even forfeit our inheritance. God's love for us will never change, but our experience of His love and our enjoyment of living with Him will be hindered when we willfully act against His love.*

Q: Is it possible to follow God and still miss out on the blessing of being His son?
- *Yes, if we keep trying to earn God's approval and blessing, we will miss out on enjoying His unconditional love and approval.*

Q: Who do you relate to within the story?
- *Just get some feedback.*

Summary

> When Jesus shared this parable, He was revealing the heart of God to us. He wasn't condemning either son for the choices they had made, but used each son to highlight a different aspect of God's love for us. The younger son wasted his life and the inheritance that God had given him. When he realized what he had done he turned back to God and found God already waiting and watching for him, with arms of love wide open. The unconditional love of God swept over the son. His old life of selfishness was washed away in the Father's love and a new life of blessing, honor, and privilege began.
>
> The elder son refused to celebrate. He had spent his life trying to earn God's blessing and approval, only to be told that he always had it. He simply had to ask for whatever he wanted and the Father would have gladly given it to him.
>
> What Jesus is revealing to us about God is that the Father loves us with an unfailing, unchanging, unshakeable love. He won't give up on us. He will keep calling us and waiting for us until we come to Him, and then He will shower us with His love.

He will accept us back into His family completely and unconditionally. As children of God, we can then enjoy all the awesome family benefits given to us by our Heavenly Father. We can live in the blessing, approval, provision, protection, authority and love of God forever.

3 | Home Reading and Questions

☐ **Isaiah 61:10**
In the Bible, clothing is often used as a metaphor to describe the reality of a person's heart.

I: Imagine what it would feel like in your heart, to be completely embraced by the Father and clothed with the garment of salvation (saving love).

Q: What does it mean to be saved by God? Saved from what?

Q: What would it be like to be lavished with God's love?

☐ **1 John 4:7-14**
I: Imagine a God, who is love. Imagine how this God thinks. How He feels. Imagine a God who can only love. Imagine this love, bursting forth in creative power at the beginning of time. Imagine this God of love, releasing His love into creation as He formed and created you.

Q: What does it mean for God to create me in love?

Q: Do I really love other people?

Q: What is love?

Q: Can God ever not love?

☐ **Matthew 5:38-48**
Q: What is Jesus revealing about God in this passage?

Q: Why does God make it rain and shine on both the righteous and the unrighteous people?

Q: What does it mean for me to love my enemies?

☐ **John 13:1-17**
I: Imagine being among the disciples. Imagine having hot, dusty, sweaty feet. Imagine Jesus, taking a towel and washing your feet.

Q: Why did Jesus wash His disciples' feet?

Q: What does Jesus reveal about God in this passage?

Q: Why did Jesus call His followers to serve each other?

☐ **Prayer** God, I'd like more love in my life. If you really are love, can you please show me your love? Can you please help me to receive your love?

☐ **John 7 - John 9**
Write down your questions here:

☐ **Experiences with God**
Write down some of your own prayers, discoveries, questions and experiences.

4 | Jesus and the Father

Leader's Notes

This study looks at the relationship between Jesus and the Father.

Key Goals
- To show how Jesus reveals the Father.
- To show how Jesus and the Father are One.
- To ask the question: is Jesus God or not?

John 14:1-11

¹"Let not your hearts be troubled. Believe in God; believe also in me. ² In my Father's house are many rooms. If it were not so, would I have told you that I go to prepare a place for you? ³ And if I go and prepare a place for you, I will come again and will take you to myself, that where I am you may be also. ⁴ And you know the way to where I am going." ⁵ Thomas said to him, "Lord, we do not know where you are going. How can we know the way?" ⁶ Jesus said to him, "I am the way, and the truth, and the life. No one comes to the Father except through me. ⁷ If you had known me, you would have known my Father also. From now on you do know him and have seen him."

⁸ Philip said to him, "Lord, show us the Father, and it is enough for us." ⁹ Jesus said to him, "Have I been with you so long, and you still do not know me, Philip? Whoever has seen me has seen the Father. How can you say, 'Show us the Father'? ¹⁰ Do you not believe that I am in the Father and the Father is in me? The words that I say to you I do not speak on my own authority, but the Father who dwells in me does his works. ¹¹ Believe me that I am in the Father and the Father is in me, or else believe on account of the works themselves."

Recap *Jesus says to the disciples not to be afraid because He will prepare a place for them. He says that He is the way, truth and life and that He is the only way to the Father. Because the disciples know Jesus, they also know the Father because the Father lives in Jesus and works through Him.*

Q: Who is the Father?
- *The Eternal Creator, the One True God.*

Q: What does Jesus mean when He says "If you had known me, you would have known my Father also" and "whoever has seen me has seen the Father"?
- *Jesus and the Father are exactly like each other.*
- *Jesus came to reveal the Father through His own life.*

Father + Son = 1

John 10:22-33

²² At that time the Feast of Dedication took place at Jerusalem. It was winter, ²³ and Jesus was walking in the temple, in the colonnade of Solomon. ²⁴ So the Jews gathered around him and said to him, "How long will you keep us in suspense? If you are the Christ, tell us plainly." ²⁵ Jesus answered them, "I told you, and you do not believe. The works that I do in my Father's name bear witness about me, ²⁶ but you do not believe because you are not among my sheep. ²⁷ My sheep hear my voice, and I know them, and they follow me. ²⁸ I give them eternal life, and they will never perish, and no one will snatch them out of my hand. ²⁹ My Father, who has given them to me, is greater than all, and no one is able to snatch them out of the Father's hand. ³⁰ I and the Father are one."

³¹ The Jews picked up stones again to stone him. ³² Jesus answered them, "I have shown you many good works from the Father; for which of them are you going to stone me?" ³³ The Jews answered him, "It is not for a good work that we are going to stone you but for blasphemy, because you, being a man, make yourself God."

Recap *The Jews ask Jesus if He is the Messiah/Christ. Jesus says that He has already told them and they don't get it because they're not His sheep (they refuse to follow Him). Jesus says that He gives eternal life and that no one can take His sheep out of the Father's hand. Jesus says that He and the Father are One. The Jews want to kill him.*

Q: What does Jesus mean when He says "I and the Father are one"?
- *That He is one with the Father. But "one" how? One nature. One heart. One mind. One substance. One being. One entity. One God.*

Q: Why did the Jews want to kill Jesus?
- *Because by saying that He gives eternal life and that He and the Father are One, Jesus is saying that He is God.*

> The Jews wanted to kill Jesus because He insisted that He was God. He was (and is) the only source of eternal life. He and the Father are One. It was not long before Jesus was killed because of His claim to be God.

Q: At the time, claiming to be God was a crime punishable by death. If Jesus was just a religious teacher and He knew that He was not actually God, why would He risk death for a lie?
- *He wouldn't. To die for a lie would mean that Jesus was totally self-deceived and even psychotic. Yet all His teachings show no sign of self-deception but rather they show profound insights into the truth. His life was a life of uncompromising love with none of the usual signs of delusion.*

> So we are left with only two valid perspectives on Jesus:
> 1. Jesus really is God and everything He said was true; or
> 2. He was insane to the point of dying for a delusion, and we cannot trust anything He said.

Q: Is this fair that there are only two positions that we can have on Jesus? Or are there other perspectives?
- *Just get some ideas.*

Son of God

Matthew 16:13-17
¹³ Now when Jesus came into the district of Caesarea Philippi, he asked his disciples, "Who do people say that the Son of Man is?" ¹⁴ And they said, "Some say John the Baptist, others say Elijah, and others Jeremiah or one of the prophets." ¹⁵ He said to them, "But who do you say that I am?" ¹⁶ Simon Peter replied, "You are the Christ, the Son of the living God." ¹⁷ And Jesus answered him, "Blessed are you, Simon Bar-Jonah! For flesh and blood has not revealed this to you, but my Father who is in heaven."

Recap *Jesus wanted to know who people thought He was. Then He wanted to know who Peter thought He was. Peter said He was the Christ, the Son of God. Jesus blessed Him because the Father in heaven had revealed it to Peter.*

Q: What does it mean for Jesus to be the Christ, the Son of the living God?
- *It means that Jesus was not only sent by God to save and lead God's people, but that Jesus shares the same nature as God, in other words, that Jesus was divine.*

God the Word with God

John 1: 1-5
¹ In the beginning was the Word, and the Word was with God, and the Word was God. ² He was in the beginning with God. ³ All things were made through him, and without him was not any thing made that was made. ⁴ In him was life, and the life was the light of men. ⁵ The light shines in the darkness, and the darkness has not overcome it.

Recap *The Word was in the beginning and was God. God made everything through the Word. In Him was life, which is our light. It shines in the darkness and can't be overcome.*

Q: How can 'the Word' be a *him?*
- *Because here the "Word" refers to Jesus Christ.*

" In this passage, John describes Jesus as the *Word of God*. The term *word* here is the Greek word *logos*, which means an expression or statement. It was used by Greek people at the time to refer to the divine but impersonal force, which governed the universe and gave all things life. A Jewish perspective was that the "Logos of the living God is the bond of everything, holding all things together…" Here John confirms that the logos is truly divine, and that the logos is the creative power of God that sustains and gives life to all things. Yet John goes a step beyond Greek thought by revealing that the divine logos is not an impersonal force but a person: the Eternal God in the person of Jesus Christ.

Read the passage again, replacing *Word* with *Jesus:*

John 1: 1-5
¹ In the beginning was Jesus, and Jesus was with God, and Jesus was God. ² He was in the beginning with God. ³ All things were made through Jesus, and without him was not any thing made that was made. ⁴ In Jesus was life, and the life was the light of men. ⁵ The light [of Jesus] shines in the darkness, and the darkness has not overcome it.

Q: How can it be that at the beginning, Jesus was with God and at the same time Jesus was God?
- *There is a unity to God. We'll look at this more later.*

Q: How can God be a person?
- *He is all-powerful. He can humble Himself to become a real person.*

Q: Why did God become a person?
- *Just get some thoughts and ideas at this point.*

Only God with God

John 1: 14-18
¹⁴ And the Word became flesh and dwelt among us, and we have seen his glory, glory as of the only Son from the Father, full of grace and truth. ¹⁵ (John bore witness about him, and cried out, "This was he of whom I said, 'He who comes after me ranks before me, because he was before me.'") ¹⁶ For from his fullness we have all received, grace upon grace. ¹⁷ For the law was given through Moses; grace and truth came through Jesus Christ. ¹⁸ No one has ever seen God; the only God, who is at the Father's side, he has made him known.

Q: Who is "the only God who is at the Father's side"?
- *Jesus.*

Q: What has He done?
- *Made God known.*

Recap *Jesus came to live with us and people saw His glory. We have grace from Jesus. Jesus is God and He is at the Father's side. He is God and with God. Only Jesus has made the Father known to us.*

> The whole Bible centers around Jesus. He reveals the Father to us, not because He has had a special insight or revelation of God, but because He is God. He and the Father are One. When we read of the life of Jesus, we see the life of God being expressed on earth. When we read His teachings, we get insight into the nature of God. Jesus is the light of revelation because He is the Light of God. The Bible simply says that Jesus is God.

Q: So who do you say Jesus is?

- *Don't force people to answer. Just note that sooner or later we need to decide how we will answer this question. Is Jesus God, or was He an insane teacher who died for His delusion?*

Summary

Through His life and His teachings, Jesus left no middle ground to stand on. Either we accept that everything He said was true, or we deny it all. By willingly dying for calling Himself God, Jesus Himself denies us the option of believing that He was just a good teacher and no more. So we simply cannot pick and choose which of His teachings we agree with. It is a case of all or nothing.

If we choose to believe that Jesus is God then we also need to think about what that means for our lives and how we should respond to Him. What does Jesus teach us about answering His call? What does He show us about what it means to follow Him?

4 | Home Reading and Questions

☐ **Colossians 1:15-20**
I: Imagine Jesus having the fullness of God dwelling within Him, cloaked in humility.

Q: All things were created through Jesus and for Him. So what does that mean for me to be created *for* Jesus?

Q: If Jesus created everything, what could I possibly give back to Him? What could I give Jesus that He doesn't already have?

Q: Do I have real peace with God?

☐ **Philippians 2:1-11**
I: Imagine Jesus existing in the form of God. Imagine Him emptying Himself and becoming a man. Imagine the Creator of the universe, humbling Himself to become a servant and to suffer death for us.

Q: Is it possible to do "nothing from selfishness"? Why?

Q: What attitude did Jesus have when He became a man?

Q: How can I have that same attitude?

☐ **Acts17:22-28**
Q: Is God far from me?

Q: What does it mean for me to "live and move and have my being" in God?

Q: If God created me then can I call myself a child of God?

☐ **Prayer** Dear God, if you're real, can you please reveal yourself to me and help me to know what it means to follow you.

☐ **John 10 - John 12**
Write down your questions here:

☐ **Experiences with God**
Write down some of your own prayers, discoveries, questions and experiences.

5 | Jesus the Reality

Leader's Notes
This study introduces Jesus as Reality.

The key goals of the study are:
- *To show how Jesus is Reality.*
- *To show how the word of God and the Spirit lead us to experience reality.*

One Way

John 14:6
Jesus said to him, "I am the way, and the truth, and the life. No one comes to the Father except through me."

Recap *Jesus is the way, truth and life. We need to come through Jesus to get to the Father.*

Q: Why is Jesus the only way to God?
- *Because Jesus is God. He and the Father are One and they cannot be separated. We cannot come to the Father unless we come to Jesus. Jesus is the living way—the only connection between people and God.*

Q: What does it mean for Jesus to be the truth?
- *Just get some ideas at this point.*

❝ In early Greek culture, the Greek word *aletheia* (truth) was used to express **reality** as opposed to fantasy or illusion. Truth is reality. So when Jesus says "I am the Truth", He is saying that He is Reality—the ultimate Reality.

Q: What does it mean for Jesus to be Reality?
- *Remember John 1: "All things came into being through Him…" All reality flows from Jesus who is the Reality. He makes everything real.*
- *There is no falseness in Jesus. Everything He says is absolutely true and real.*

Q: If Jesus is Reality, what does it mean to live apart from Jesus?
- *What's the opposite of reality? Fantasy or deception. Apart from Jesus we can only live in a spiritual fantasy.*

Q: What does it mean to live in a fantasy?
- *We believe lies. We believe what the world tells us instead of what God says is true. God offers truth, the world offers lies and half-truths. God offers the reality of joy, the world offers the fantasy of entertainment. God calls us to live in His love, the world says that love is really just lust. God calls us to join Him in humility, while the world celebrates the proud. To live apart from Jesus is to be ignorant of God and all the blessing that He wants to pour out into our lives. It is to be ignorant of God's design and purpose for our lives.*

Q: In the story of the Father's love, did the younger son live in the reality or fantasy?
- *Fantasy. He pursued his own desires and disconnected from the reality of his own identity and his father's love.*

Q: Was the fantasy enjoyable?
- *Maybe for a while it was an enjoyable waste of time. But ultimately, no. He enjoyed fleeting lust rather than lasting love. He enjoyed temporal indulgence rather than lasting provision. He enjoyed momentary entertainment rather than lasting joy. And when times got hard, the enjoyment was just a memory and he was reduced to nothing. So maybe the question is not so much about whether or not reality is more enjoyable than fantasy. Maybe the question should be about which option ultimately leads to life, love and truth? Reality in Jesus or fantasy in the world?*

Q: Do we want to live in reality?
- *Explore this a little. What do people really want spiritually?*
- *Would living in the Reality of Jesus be better or worse/ easier or harder than living in a spiritual fantasy?*

Word of Reality

John 17:13-17 – Jesus prays to the Father
[13] "But now I am coming to you, and these things I speak in the world, that they may have my joy fulfilled in themselves. [14] I have given them your word, and the world has hated them because they are not of the world, just as I am not of the world. [15] I do not ask that you take them out of the world, but that you keep them from the evil one. [16] They are not of the world, just as I am not of the world. [17] Sanctify them in the truth; your word is truth."

Recap *Jesus prays that His disciples may have joy and be protected in the world. He asks the Father to sanctify them in the truth and says that God's word is truth.*

The word *sanctify* means to set apart and make pure. So Jesus is praying that God would set His people apart and purify them by His word of truth.

Q: God's word is truth and reality. What does that tell us about the Bible?
- *That the Bible reveals what is true so we can trust what it says. The Bible isn't just about philosophy or theory but reality. It's not trying to communicate an intellectual understanding of God but to reveal the reality of God to us.*
- *The truth of God is written in the Bible for our benefit, precisely so that we might be empowered to enter the reality that it reveals. For example, the Bible speaks of God's forgiveness so that we might have the confidence to receive the forgiveness of God. Everything is written in the Bible to empower us to experience more of the reality of God's love and design for us.*

Spirit of Reality

John 14:16-17
¹⁶ And I will ask the Father, and he will give you another Helper, to be with you forever, ¹⁷ even the Spirit of truth, whom the world cannot receive, because it neither sees him nor knows him. You know him, for he dwells with you and will be in you.

Recap *Jesus will send the Spirit of truth to Help us and be with us.*

John 16:13
¹³ When the Spirit of truth comes, he will guide you into all the truth, for he will not speak on his own authority, but whatever he hears he will speak, and he will declare to you the things that are to come.

Recap *When the Spirit of truth comes He will guide us into all truth because He will speak what He hears.*

> In terms of truth and reality, these verses show that Jesus has promised to give us the Spirit of Reality who will help us and guide us into reality. He will live within us and speak whatever God tells Him, and show us what He is leading us into. In this way, God does not leave us just with His word telling us about the truth. He gives us His Spirit to help us to experience the reality of His truth.

Q: What's the difference between learning about God's love and experiencing the reality of His love?
- *We can learn about love and come to an intellectual understanding of it. But that doesn't mean that we really know His love. When we experience God's love then it becomes real for us.*

Q: Do we want to experience the reality of God's love?
- *Get some responses here.*

Romans 5:1-5
¹ Therefore, since we have been justified by faith, we have peace with God through our Lord Jesus Christ. ² Through him we have also obtained access by faith into this grace in which we stand, and we rejoice in hope of the glory of God. ³ Not only that, but we rejoice in our sufferings, knowing that suffering produces endurance, ⁴ and endurance produces character, and character produces hope, ⁵ and hope does not put us to shame, because God's love has been poured into our hearts through the Holy Spirit who has been given to us.

Recap *We have peace with God through Jesus. We gained access by faith into His grace. We celebrate our sufferings because it produces endurance, character and hope, and we have no shame, because God's love has been poured into our hearts through the Holy Spirit.*

Q: We can learn about God's love in the Bible, but we can only experience His love poured into our hearts through His Holy Spirit. So if we can only receive the love of God through the Holy Spirit then who or what is the Spirit?
- *Get some ideas.*

 Jesus has lots of different names. He is called Immanuel, the Prince of Peace, the Alpha and Omega, the Son of Man etc. Likewise, the Holy Spirit is also known by different names such as the Spirit of Truth, the Spirit of God, and the Spirit of Jesus.

As humans, we have been created with a heart, soul, mind and body. Our body is a container for our material life (like our blood, bones, muscles and organs). Our mind is a container for our thoughts. And our heart (spiritual not physical) is a container for our spirit, which is the substance of our inner nature and character. When we receive the Holy Spirit, He fills our hearts with His presence and He redefines our inner nature and character. It's like our heart becomes a shared space with the Spirit of Jesus. When the Spirit of Jesus dwells within us, we automatically start to share in and experience the reality of Jesus. Because His own Spirit is within us, Jesus shares His love with us and pours it out into our hearts. His love then changes us. It changes our nature and character. It changes the way we think, how we feel, our intentions and motivations, and ultimately our actions.

Imagining the Impossible

1 Corinthians 2:9-16
⁹ But, as it is written— What no eye has seen, nor ear heard, nor the heart of man imagined, what God has prepared for those who love him"— ¹⁰ these things God has revealed to us through the Spirit. For the Spirit searches everything, even the depths of God. ¹¹ For who knows a person's thoughts except the spirit of that person, which is in him? So also no one comprehends the thoughts of God except the Spirit of God. ¹² Now we have received not the spirit of the world, but the Spirit who is from God, that we might understand the things freely given us by God. ¹³ And we impart this in words not taught by human wisdom but taught by the Spirit, interpreting spiritual truths to those who are spiritual.

¹⁴ The natural person does not accept the things of the Spirit of God, for they are folly to him, and he is not able to understand them because they are spiritually discerned. ¹⁵ The spiritual person judges all things, but is himself to be judged by no one. ¹⁶ "For who has understood the mind of the Lord so as to instruct him?" But we have the mind of Christ.

Recap *God has prepared better things for us than we could possibly imagine. Only the Spirit of God knows God's thoughts and we have received His Spirit so that we might know what God has freely given us. The natural person can't accept or understand the things of God. But we have the mind of Christ.*

Q: What has God prepared for those who love Him?
- *More than we can imagine.*

Q: Why does God give us His Spirit?
- *That we might know the things that God has freely given us.*
- *That we might know the thoughts of God.*

Just as God gives us His Spirit so that He can share His heart with us, so He also gives us His Spirit so that He can share His mind with us. No one can possibly know the thoughts of God except for the Spirit of God. So God gives us His Spirit to share His thoughts with us and reveal the awesome things that God has prepared for us. These things are our inheritance in Jesus: they are the blessings, gifts, love, power and times of transformation that we experience as we take possession of our spiritual inheritance.

Ephesians 3:20-21
[20] Now to him who is able to do far more abundantly than all that we ask or think, according to the power at work within us, [21] to him be glory in the church and in Christ Jesus throughout all generations, forever and ever. Amen.

Q: What can God do for us?
- *More than we could possibly imagine.*
- *So dare to imagine. Dare to dream about what God might do for us and in us.*

Summary

 Truth is reality and Jesus is the ultimate truth. Everything that is real flows from the reality of Jesus. He is life and gives life. Jesus is the centre, source and sustainer of reality.

To live more in the truth is to live in deeper connection and relationship with Jesus. It is to experience more of the life, love, nature, presence and power of Jesus Christ.

The word of God describes the reality that is found in Jesus. Because God's word is truth, the experiences we have of God will always be consistent with the word. It is the standard of reality. It is the foundation for our experience.

To lead us into reality, God has given us His Spirit. The Spirit of God takes the truth of the word and leads us into the personal experience of that truth. Through His Spirit, Jesus also shares His heart and His mind with us. When the Spirit of Jesus dwells within us, He pours out the love of God into us and shares the thoughts of God with us.

5 | Home Reading and Questions

☐ **Psalm 139:17-18** *This is a song, written by King David of Israel.*
Q: How did David know the thoughts of God?

Q: Why were God's thoughts so precious to David?

Q: Would God want to share His thoughts with me?

I: Imagine a God of love whose thoughts are so vast they are impossible to count. Imagine Him thinking about you. Imagine Him sharing some of His thoughts with you.

☐ **Ephesians 3:14-21**
I: Imagine a love that surpasses knowledge. Imagine being the object of that love.

Q: What does it mean to be filled with God?

Q: Can God really do abundantly more than I could ask or think?

Q: What is the limit of my imagination? If I could ask God for anything, what would I ask for?

☐ **Romans 8:28-30**
Q: How can God make everything work out for good?

Q: Would God want to make everything in my life work out for good?

Q: What does it mean to be conformed to the image of God's Son?

☐ **Prayer** God, if you are real, I'd like to know what you have prepared for me. Please share your thoughts with me and show me something of the life you'd like to give me.

☐ John 13 - John 15
Write down your questions here:

☐ Experiences with God
Write down some of your own prayers, discoveries, questions and experiences.

6 | Image of God

Leader's Notes
This study looks more at how Jesus is the exact image of God and how we are created in His image. Note: this study is longer than usual so try to keep things moving without rushing.

Key Goals
- To show how Jesus is the image of God.
- To show how God created us to live in unity with Him.

Colossians 1:15-20
[15] He [Jesus] is the image of the invisible God, the firstborn of all creation. [16] For by him all things were created, in heaven and on earth, visible and invisible, whether thrones or dominions or rulers or authorities—all things were created through him and for him. [17] And he is before all things, and in him all things hold together.

Recap *Jesus is the image of the invisible God. Through Jesus everything was created through Him and for Him. Everything holds together in Him.*

Q: What is an image?
- *It's like a picture or photograph or video. It captures a scene exactly as it was at the time.*

Q: What does it mean for Jesus to be the image of God?
- *Jesus is like a living photograph of God. He is exactly like God. The nature and heart and will of God are present and can all be perfectly seen in Jesus.*

Q: How can Jesus be God, but also be the image of God? Isn't an image a copy?
- *Remember John 1, Jesus is with God, and He is God. He is the "only God, who is at the Father's side." There is an unimaginable kind of unity here between God the Father and Jesus the Son. Jesus and the Father share one Spirit—they are One in essence and being. Their unity is so perfect and complete that the Bible is true when it says that Jesus is God and at the same time He is with God. This principle is the same for God's image. Jesus is both the image of God and God Himself.*
- *Don't worry if this seems a little difficult to get your head around. Remember that God exists beyond the heavens and is greater than we can possibly understand. Our minds are never, ever, going to come to a complete understanding of God. So it is with the relationship within God Himself. Our understanding of how the Father and Son can be One and yet distinct, will always be imperfect. Thankfully, our experience of God's saving love does not depend on our intellectual understanding of the truth. It just requires an open heart.*

Created in His Image

Genesis 1:26
²⁶ Then God said, "Let us make man in our image, after our likeness. And let them have dominion over the fish of the sea and over the birds of the heavens and over the livestock and over all the earth and over every creeping thing that creeps on the earth."

Recap *God said "Let us make man in our image and let them rule over all the rest of creation."*

Q: Who does "us" refer to?
- *God the Father and Jesus the Son. God is talking to Himself.*

Q: What was God's design for people?
- *He created us in His image and likeness, so we would have His heart and life within us.*
- *We were created to show the love of God in the world.*

Q: If Jesus is the image of God then what does it mean to be designed in His image?
- *We are created to be like Jesus. How can we be like Jesus?*
- *We are designed to have the nature of Jesus within us and to live in unity with Him.*

> When God created people, He didn't make a copy of His nature of love and place it in the heart of man. Instead He created people to exist in unity with Him, sharing the heart and nature of Jesus.
>
> To separate the qualities of God's nature from Jesus Christ is like trying to separate the breath in our lungs from the air around us. We do not take a breath from the atmosphere and call it our own and then try to hold onto it forever. Rather we share the air around us, continually breathing it in and releasing it out. The air within us is united with the air around us.
>
> In the same way, we do not receive love from God and then separate that love from Him by calling it our own. On the contrary, the presence of God's love in our hearts connects us to the Source. Like air, God's love is the basis of our unity with Him and it needs to continually flow back to Him. In this way, to be created in the image of God is not to be created just as a reflection of God, but to be created in unity with God. It is to have His nature alive within us, being expressed through our words and actions of love.

Q: What does it mean to live in unity with Jesus?
- *To share His nature with Him. To share His love. To share His heart. To share His mind. To share His will. To share His strength. To live and work and play with Him.*

Q: If we are all created in the image of God then is everyone living according to God's image?
- *Sadly no. God is love and so very few people live out God's love.*

Q: Why? What happened to the divine image in people?
- *Get some ideas.*

An Image Lost

Romans 1:16-25
[16] For I am not ashamed of the gospel, for it is the power of God for salvation to everyone who believes, to the Jew first and also to the Greek. [17] For in it the righteousness of God is revealed from faith for faith, as it is written, "The righteous shall live by faith."

[18] For the wrath of God is revealed from heaven against all ungodliness and unrighteousness of men, who by their unrighteousness suppress the truth. [19] For what can be known about God is plain to them, because God has shown it to them. [20] For his invisible attributes, namely, his eternal power and divine nature, have been clearly perceived, ever since the creation of the world, in the things that have been made. So they are without excuse. [21] For although they knew God, they did not honor him as God or give thanks to him, but they became futile in their thinking, and their foolish hearts were darkened. [22] Claiming to be wise, they became fools, [23] and exchanged the glory of the immortal God for images resembling mortal man and birds and animals and creeping things.

[24] Therefore God gave them up in the lusts of their hearts to impurity, to the dishonoring of their bodies among themselves, [25] because they exchanged the truth about God for a lie and worshiped and served the creature rather than the Creator, who is blessed forever! Amen.

Recap *The gospel is the power of God. The wrath of God is against all ungodliness and unrighteousness. Since the creation of the world, everyone has known about God's power and His divine nature through His creation and so no one has any excuse for* *ignoring God. Everyone has had an inner-knowledge in their hearts about God, but in the past people did not honor or acknowledge God. Instead we exchanged the glory of God's image for the image of mortal man and we swapped truth for a lie. So God gave us over to the new image we created. The result was that we were filled with dishonorable passions and had corrupt hearts that were full of lust and pride.*

Q: What is this passage saying about the image of God in man?
- *That ever since creation, every person has known about God and His nature.*
- *That we lost the divine image. People traded the image of God for a different image.*
- *That we stopped worshiping God and started to worship ourselves. Instead of living in His love, we lived in selfishness, lust and impurity.*

Q: What impact did the choice to sin have on the identity of people?
- *We created a new identity for ourselves.*
- *We separated our identity from God.*
- *We became something other than what God designed.*

"
God's image is love and the opposite of love isn't hate. It's selfishness. When we traded the image of God for our own image, we began to live for ourselves rather than for God. We abandoned God's ways so we could make our own way. We did not want to be told who we were or what we should do. We wanted to be independent and answerable to no one. So we gave up God's design for our lives and created our own identity. We made ourselves our god.

The big problem with this was that by rejecting the image of God, we rejected Jesus and broke our unity with Him. We disconnected from our Creator, which meant that we lost the power of His love within us and became enslaved to self. Without the love of God in our hearts, we weren't able to act according to God's image. We could try to be loving, but ultimately we were powerless to overcome our own selfishness and truly live in selfless love.

Q: Romans 1:18 says that God's wrath is revealed against all ungodliness and unrighteousness. What is unrighteousness and ungodliness? Why does God's intense anger burn towards unrighteousness and ungodliness?
- *Get some ideas.*

" According to the Bible, *righteousness* is the approval of God that comes from trusting in Him and expressing His love. It is acting *right* in God's sight because we possess and express His nature of pure love. To be *unrighteous* is to lack the love of God and to act against His love. Such action is also called *sin.* Sin covers all non-loving action, from the more serious acts such as murder, rape, adultery and abuse, to less violent acts such lying, stealing, manipulating and degrading others. Regardless of the nature of the act, all sin ultimately finds its source in selfishness. Selfishness, not hatred, is the true opposite of love. So regardless of what we do, we live in *unrighteousness, ungodliness* and *sin* simply when we live selfishly.

Light does not accommodate darkness. Instead, when we turn the lights on, the darkness disappears. In the same way, love cannot accommodate evil—love must overcome and destroy all sin, evil and selfishness. This is why the wrath of God burns against unrighteousness and ungodliness. God hates everything that opposes His love and His design for us.

Q: So where does that leave us? Does the anger of God burn against us for following our selfish ways or does the love of God burn for us?
- *Just get some ideas. Be careful not to let people feel that God hates them. The end conclusion is that God has made a way for us to experience His awesome love, despite our sin. Questions to possibly consider:*
- *Is the anger of God against evil in conflict with His love for His creation?*
- *Isn't God's wrath towards evil a quality of a love that cannot tolerate sin?*
- *Why does God require us to account for our sin? Can't He just make everyone sin-free and pure?*
- *Why did God even let us become selfish? This comes down to the idea of choice—the choice to love God or to reject His love. Why is choice important?*

- *How much is selfishness a part of our identity? If we viewed sin as a spiritual cancer, would we still consider it to be an engrained part of who we are?*
- *Can we imagine God unleashing His anger and consuming our selfishness, while at the same time unleashing His awesome love and setting us free to be filled with His love?*

Summary

> Jesus Christ is the image of God. The essence and nature and power of God are found in Jesus Christ. When God created people, He created us in His image and likeness. He designed us to live in a unity of love with Jesus Christ Himself.
>
> So when God the Father created us, He created us through Jesus and specifically *for* Him. We were not created to be our own. Yet every single person throughout all history has chosen to go their own way. We have all denied the purpose of God for our lives and chosen self over love.
>
> When we chose to make our own way in life, we corrupted God's image within us. We traded His eternal love for temporal lust. We swapped truth for a lie and embraced fantasy over reality. We denied God and become self-conscious instead of God-conscious. The result was that we became enslaved to this thing called 'self'. Self ruled over us. It forced us to act upon our selfish passions and desires. Self became our god, and despite all the benefits and successes that putting self first brings in life, none of it can fill the void within our hearts. Every one of us has a need that can only be filled by one thing: the love of God.

6 | Home Reading and Questions

☐ **Hebrews 1:1-3**
Q: What does it mean for Jesus to be the radiance of God's glory?

Q: What does it mean for Jesus to be the exact representation (imprint/likeness) of God's nature?

Q: What does it mean for Jesus to uphold (or sustain) all things by His word?

☐ **Matthew 17:1-3**
I: Imagine being with Peter, James and John, and seeing Jesus reveal Himself. Imagine watching Jesus radiate God's glory, with His face shining like the sun, and His clothes white as light. Imagine God coming as a cloud of light, speaking of His love for Jesus and calling us to listen to Jesus.

Q: How could Jesus change Himself into light?

Q: What does it mean for Jesus to be the "light of life"? (see John 1)

Q: What would be my response if I saw Jesus reveal Himself as light?

Q: How would that change me?

☐ **Ephesians 4:17-24**
Q: What does it mean to be darkened in my understanding?

Q: What have I given myself up to?

Q: What is the old self? What is it like?

Q: What is the new self? What is it like?

Q: Who am I? Does my identity flow from my old self, my new self, or both?

Q: Who has God created me to be?

☐ **Prayer** Jesus, if you are light, could you please bring light to my life? Can you help me to see who you created me to be?

☐ **John 16 - John 17**
Write down your questions here:

☐ Experiences with God
Write down some of your own prayers, discoveries, questions and experiences.

7 | Paying the Debt

Leader's Notes
This study looks more at how our sin creates a life-debt with God.

Key Goals
- To show how our sin and selfishness creates a debt we can't possibly hope to repay.
- To show how sin leads to death.
- To show how Jesus took our debt at the cross and paid it for us.

Colossians 1:15-20
[15] He [Jesus] is the image of the invisible God, the firstborn of all creation. [16] For by him all things were created, in heaven and on earth, visible and invisible, whether thrones or dominions or rulers or authorities—all things were created through him and for him. [17] And he is before all things, and in him all things hold together.

Recap *Jesus is the image of the invisible God. Through Jesus everything was created through Him and for Him. Everything holds together in Him.*

Q: What does it mean for everything to be created for Jesus?
- *God the Father created everything to be a blessing for Jesus.*
- *All creation, including us, was designed to be an expression of God's love for Jesus.*

Q: What does it mean to be created as an expression of the Father's love for Jesus?
- *It means that we are designed to be living channels of the Father's love for Jesus. See John 17:26.*

- *God intended that our entire lives would be defined by love. We were created to overflow with the love of God, and to live in love, moment by moment, in every detail and circumstance of life.*

> God created people to live in His image as vessels of His love for Jesus. We were designed to be channels through which the love of God would always flow. Yet we all rejected God's image for our lives and chose selfishness over love. By living for self, we closed our hearts to God's love. Instead of being vessels of the Creator and His love, we became vessels of self, sin, brokenness and corruption.

Psalm 53:1-3
¹ The fool says in his heart, "There is no God."
　　they are corrupt, doing abominable iniquity;
　　there is none who does good.
² God looks down from heaven
　　on the children of man
　　to see if there are any who understand,
　　who seek after God.
³ They have all fallen away;
　　together they have become corrupt;
　　there is none who does good,
　　not even one.

Recap *Only foolish people think there is no God. There is no one who does good. God looked down to see if anyone would seek after God, but we had all fallen away and were all corrupt.*

Q: Has anyone ever lived their entire life in God's image?
- *Everyone has drifted from God's design and we have all gone our own way. No one has ever lived their entire life for God. Everyone has fallen short of God's design for our lives. We have all chosen self over God.*

Romans 6:20-23
[20] For when you were slaves of sin, you were free in regard to righteousness. [21] But what fruit were you getting at that time from the things of which you are now ashamed? For the end of those things is death. [22] But now that you have been set free from sin and have become slaves of God, the fruit you get leads to sanctification and its end, eternal life. [23] For the wages of sin is death, but the free gift of God is eternal life in Christ Jesus our Lord.

Recap *When we were enslaved to sin, it led to nothing good for us. Instead it led us into death. Now we are set free, and are enslaved (or bonded) to God, which leads to eternal life.*

Q: What does it mean "wages of sin"?
- *It is the inescapable result of sin, both now and eternally. Sin leads to death.*
- *So what does it mean by death?*

Sin as a Weighty Debt

The Bible likens sin to a weight, a crime, and a debt. The weight of sin is the burden that we carry when we know in our hearts that we've done wrong. It is the weight of an ongoing spiritual death—of not being right with God and united with Him.

Sin is also like a crime because when we sin we break God's divine Law of Love. If we commit a crime in society, we are forced to accept the consequences. In the same way, when we sin, our actions mean that we are bound to suffer the sentence required by law for those actions. By acting selfishly we have broken God's law and we will have to face the inevitable consequence for our actions.

Finally, the Bible also likens sin to a debt that needs to be paid. As God's creation we have been made for Jesus and so we owe Him our lives—all our time, everything we are and have, it was all created to be an instrument of love for Jesus. We never had the right to abandon our purpose and take our lives away from Jesus. By going our own way, we stole our lives from God. When God created us, He invested such power and value in us that to waste our lives incurs an immeasurable debt with God. Every moment that we live for ourselves, every time we act selfishly, every time we sin, we incur an ever greater life-debt with God.

Psalm 40:5-9
⁵ Why should I fear in times of trouble, when the iniquity of those who cheat me surrounds me,
⁶ those who trust in their wealth and boast of the abundance of their riches?
⁷ Truly no man can ransom another, or give to God the price of his life,
⁸ for the ransom of their life is costly and can never suffice,
⁹ that he should live on forever and never see the pit.

Recap: *Why should we fear when people who trust in material wealth surround us? Their wealth cannot buy back their lives. They cannot repay their life-debt to God.*

Q: What does it mean to ransom a life?
- *To give God the cost of our life. To pay the debt that we owe Him.*

Q: What does the ransom purchase?
- *Eternal life rather than death.*
- *What is eternal life? A life in His image and design.*

Q: Is there any way we can ransom our own lives?
- *We can't overcome or atone for our sin and selfishness. Nothing we could do could ever earn eternal life. No amount of good works will ever restore us to the image of God. No amount of prayer or worship or giving or serving or anything can ever ransom our lives and return us to the image of God. Nothing we can do can repay the debt we owe God.*

Q: So how can we get right with God? How can the debt be paid?
- *There is nothing we can do to get right with God. Only He can pay our debt for us.*

Life-Debt Nailed

Colossians 2: 8-15

⁸ See to it that no one takes you captive by philosophy and empty deceit, according to human tradition, according to the elemental spirits of the world, and not according to Christ. ⁹ For in him the whole fullness of deity dwells bodily, ¹⁰ and you have been filled in him, who is the head of all rule and authority. ¹¹ In him also you were circumcised with a circumcision made without hands, by putting off the body of the flesh, by the circumcision of Christ, ¹² having been buried with him in baptism, in which you were also raised with him through faith in the powerful working of God, who raised him from the dead. ¹³ And you, who were dead in your trespasses and the uncircumcision of your flesh, God made alive together with him, having forgiven us all our trespasses, ¹⁴ by canceling the record of debt that stood against us with its legal demands. This he set aside, nailing it to the cross. ¹⁵ He disarmed the rulers and authorities and put them to open shame, by triumphing over them in him.

Recap *Make sure no one deceives you with a teaching that isn't true to Jesus. The fullness of God dwells within Jesus. We were circumcised with Him through baptism and raised with Him. We were dead in our sins, but God forgave us and made us alive with Him. God cancelled the record of debt by nailing it to the cross. He defeated the rulers and authorities, triumphing over them through Jesus.*

Q: What is the record of debt that stood against us with all of its legal commands?
- *It is the debt of sin that we owe God. It is the debt that we have incurred because of our failure to keep the law of Love. It is the debt that we owe to God for all the time that we lived for ourselves and failed to live in His image. It is the debt that we could never pay.*

Q: What does it mean to have that debt cancelled?
- *We don't owe God the debt anymore. We are free from the weight and debt of sin.*

Q: How was it cancelled out?

- *It was nailed to the cross. It was cancelled out when Jesus died on the cross. The death that our sin led to and demanded was paid for by the death of Jesus.*

Q: What happened at the cross?

- *Just get some ideas...We'll look more at the cross in the next study.*

We live in a world which offers us wealth, pleasure and entertainment as its highest rewards. We live in a world that exalts material success; in a world that denies a Creator and sacrifices the love of God on the altar of self. We live in a world that considers sin normal, even healthy. We live in a world which refuses to accept any moral standard, where lust reigns and love for others is redefined as tolerance.

Because the voice of the world is constantly preaching to us, it is hard not to let it affect our thinking on sin. When so many people consider lying as a useful tool in life, it can be hard to see lying for what it is: a cold denial of the God of Truth and His image within us. In almost every aspect, we too easily fail to recognize the true nature of sin and the debt it incurs. We justify our choices to ourselves, but the truth remains: sin breaks the heart of our Creator, distorts His image within us, and incurs a life-debt that we cannot possibly hope to repay.

Forgiving the Debt

Matthew 18:23-35
²³ "Therefore the kingdom of heaven may be compared to a king who wished to settle accounts with his servants. ²⁴ When he began to settle, one was brought to him who owed him ten thousand talents. ²⁵ And since he could not pay, his master ordered him to be sold, with his wife and children and all that he had, and payment to be made. ²⁶ So the servant fell on his knees, imploring him, 'Have patience with me, and I will pay you everything.' ²⁷ And out of pity for him, the master of that servant released him and forgave him the debt. ²⁸ But when that same servant went out, he found one of his fellow servants who owed him a hundred denarii, and seizing him, he began to

choke him, saying, 'Pay what you owe.' [29] So his fellow servant fell down and pleaded with him, 'Have patience with me, and I will pay you.' [30] He refused and went and put him in prison until he should pay the debt. [31] When his fellow servants saw what had taken place, they were greatly distressed, and they went and reported to their master all that had taken place. [32] Then his master summoned him and said to him, 'You wicked servant! I forgave you all that debt because you pleaded with me. [33] And should not you have had mercy on your fellow servant, as I had mercy on you?' [34] And in anger his master delivered him to the jailers, until he should pay all his debt. [35] So also my heavenly Father will do to every one of you, if you do not forgive your brother from your heart."

Recap *A man has a debt that he can't pay. His master ordered him to be sold into slavery, but the man begged for mercy and his master forgave his debt. But the man then went to someone who owed him money and demanded payment. That person couldn't pay, and he begged for mercy, but none was given. The master heard about it and got really angry because his servant didn't show the same mercy that he had been shown. So the master restored the original debt and had his servant thrown in jail. The message is that God has forgiven us a debt that is greater than we could possibly imagine, so we should forgive everyone else for everything they do.*

" It is interesting to note here that 10,000 talents would take 200,000 years for a laborer to earn. In other words, it was a debt that there was no possibility of paying off. In contrast, the debt of 200 denarii would have taken around seven months for a laborer to earn. The high value of the talents speaks of the value that God has invested in our lives. As creations and channels of His love, each and every one of us is valued by God more than we could possibly comprehend.

Q: What does this say about the life-debt that we owe God?
- *When we were created we were entrusted with an immeasurably precious gift from God—our lives. As vessels of love, our lives our worth more to God than we could ever imagine.*
- *When we chose to follow our own ways, we wasted that gift and so incurred a debt that we could never, ever hope to repay.*

Q: What does it say about the heart of God?
- *That He is merciful and loving. That He is forgiving. That if we turn to him, and ask for forgiveness that He will totally and utterly forgive us the life-debt that we owe Him, in its entirety.*

Q: What does God require of us when He forgives us?
- *That we genuinely forgive other people.*
- *What if we feel that we can't forgive someone? Forgiveness is not a feeling, it is a decision. In order to truly forgive others, often we will need to ask God to empower us to forgive. He will be faithful to help us with this and change our hearts to forgive others.*
- *What if we don't want to forgive others? Then ask: do we want to want to forgive? If we want the desire to forgive then we can ask God to form that in our hearts and He will do it.*

Summary

No one has ever lived their lives entirely for Jesus. Everyone has embraced sin and self, and rejected the image of God for their lives. Everyone has incurred a debt that no one could possibly repay. So we all chose to live in a fantasy, denying the debt of sin and instead justifying our actions to each other. But sin is too grave to embrace as a human weakness. Sin is an extreme offense to the God of Love. It is an ongoing denial of who God created us to be and the purpose and value He infused within us at our creation. All sin is theft—theft of the time and life that God created to be spent on loving Jesus and sharing His love with people.

Thankfully God sent Jesus to overcome our sin. Through Jesus' sacrifice, God forgives the debt of everyone who calls on His mercy and love. The record of our offenses against God is taken away by Jesus, erased entirely at the cross. Through Jesus, we can know the reality of being declared truly innocent of any sin before God.

7 | Home Reading and Questions

☐ **Matthew 18:1-9, Matthew 5:27-30**
Q: Why is it so bad to lead someone to sin?

Q: Why is sin so serious?

Q: How can we truly appreciate the gravity of sin?

Note that Jesus is not saying that we should literally and physically dismember ourselves to keep ourselves from sinning. As He says in Matthew 5, the source of sin is a corrupt heart, and entertaining the corrupt desires of the heart is as bad as actually committing them. Sin is a condition of the heart. In saying that we should cut off our hands and tear out our eyes, He is painting a graphic picture of the horror of sin. Jesus is trying to communicate how serious sin is and how damaging it is to us. If we cannot understand the serious nature of sin then we will never appreciate the real extent of the spiritual debt that our sin incurs.

☐ **Romans 3: 21-26**
Q: Why is it that everyone has sinned and fallen short of living the life that God designed?

Q: In what ways have I sinned?

Q: Would God forgive anyone at all? What about really evil people? Could they be forgiven as well?

Q: What does it mean to be justified by God?

☐ **Isaiah 55:6-7**
Q: What does it mean to seek God?

Q: What does it mean for me to forsake my unrighteous ways and thoughts?

Q: What will happen if I return to God?

Q: What does it mean for God to abundantly pardon me?

I: Imagine what it would feel like to have every sin washed away. Imagine what it would feel like to be totally forgiven and know that God fully loves and accepts you.

☐ **Luke 19:1-10**
Q: If I believe in Jesus, am I free from the consequences of my sin? If I have stolen from someone or lied to them, or mistreated someone, can I forget about all those things and pretend I didn't do them?

Q: What can I do for other people that would help to repair the damage my sin has caused for them?

☐ **Prayer** God, the Bible says that you will forgive anyone that asks for your mercy and love, even me. Can you help me to really believe that? I know there are people I need to forgive. Could you help me to forgive these people?

☐ **John 18-20**
Write down your questions here:

☐ **Experiences with God**
Write down some of your own prayers, discoveries, questions and experiences.

8 | The Cross

Leader's Notes
This study looks more at how Jesus became the sacrifice to take away sin.

Key Goals
- To show how Jesus took away sin at the cross, securing our forgiveness forever.
- To show what it means to have faith in Jesus.

Mark 15:1-39 (it's a long reading so share it around if needed)
¹ And as soon as it was morning, the chief priests held a consultation with the elders and scribes and the whole council. And they bound Jesus and led him away and delivered him over to Pilate. ² And Pilate asked him, "Are you the King of the Jews?" And he answered him, "You have said so." ³ And the chief priests accused him of many things. ⁴ And Pilate again asked him, "Have you no answer to make? See how many charges they bring against you." ⁵ But Jesus made no further answer, so that Pilate was amazed.

⁶ Now at the feast he used to release for them one prisoner for whom they asked. ⁷ And among the rebels in prison, who had committed murder in the insurrection, there was a man called Barabbas. ⁸ And the crowd came up and began to ask Pilate to do as he usually did for them. ⁹ And he answered them, saying, "Do you want me to release for you the King of the Jews?" ¹⁰ For he perceived that it was out of envy that the chief priests had delivered him up. ¹¹ But the chief priests stirred up the crowd to have him release for them Barabbas instead. ¹² And Pilate again said to them, "Then what shall I do with the man you call the King of the Jews?" ¹³ And they cried out again, "Crucify him." ¹⁴ And Pilate said to them, "Why, what evil has he done?" But they shouted all the more, "Crucify him." ¹⁵ So Pilate, wishing to satisfy the crowd, released for them Barabbas, and having scourged Jesus, he delivered him to be crucified.

⁶ And the soldiers led him away inside the palace (that is, the governor's headquarters), and they called together the whole battalion. ¹⁷ And they clothed him in a purple cloak, and twisting together a crown of thorns, they put it on him. ¹⁸ And they began to salute him, "Hail, King of the Jews!" ¹⁹ And they were striking his head with a reed and spitting on him and kneeling down in homage to him. ²⁰ And when they had mocked him, they stripped him of the purple cloak and put his own clothes on him. And they led him out to crucify him.

²¹ And they compelled a passerby, Simon of Cyrene, who was coming in from the country, the father of Alexander and Rufus, to carry his cross. ²² And they brought him to the place called Golgotha (which means Place of a Skull). ²³ And they offered him wine mixed with myrrh, but he did not take it. ²⁴ And they crucified him and divided his garments among them, casting lots for them, to decide what each should take. ²⁵ And it was the third hour when they crucified him. ²⁶ And the inscription of the charge against him read, "The King of the Jews." ²⁷ And with him they crucified two robbers, one on his right and one on his left. ²⁹ And those who passed by derided him, wagging their heads and saying, "Aha! You who would destroy the temple and rebuild it in three days, ³⁰ save yourself, and come down from the cross!" ³¹ So also the chief priests with the scribes mocked him to one another, saying, "He saved others; he cannot save himself. ³² Let the Christ, the King of Israel, come down now from the cross that we may see and believe." Those who were crucified with him also reviled him.

³³ And when the sixth hour had come, there was darkness over the whole land until the ninth hour. ³⁴ And at the ninth hour Jesus cried with a loud voice, "Eloi, Eloi, lema sabachthani?" which means, "My God, my God, why have you forsaken me?" ³⁵ And some of the bystanders hearing it said, "Behold, he is calling Elijah." ³⁶ And someone ran and filled a sponge with sour wine, put it on a reed and gave it to him to drink, saying, "Wait, let us see whether Elijah will come to take him down." ³⁷ And Jesus uttered a loud cry and breathed his last. ³⁸ And the curtain of the temple was torn in two, from top to bottom. ³⁹ And when the centurion, who stood facing him, saw that in this way he breathed his last, he said, "Truly this man was the Son of God!"

Recap *Jesus was questioned by Pilate, who tried to release Him, but the people convinced him to crucify Jesus. Jesus was then abused and humiliated by the soldiers. They made someone else carry his cross. They offered Jesus some wine mixed with* *myrrh (as a sedative) but he refused it. They crucified him. They gambled for his clothes. People mocked him as he hung on the cross. Jesus called out to God. Someone gave him some sour wine (vinegar) to drink. He then cried out and died. The curtain in the temple tore in two. A soldier watching said that Jesus really was the Son of God.*

Q: Had Jesus done anything evil, worthy of death?
- *No, Jesus had done no evil. Pilate could find no reason to execute Him. The crowd could give no reason. Jesus lived His entire life for God, in His image.*

Q: Why did the people want Jesus killed?
- *The chief priests stirred up the crowd. They wanted to kill Jesus because He claimed to be God.*

Q: Did Jesus die willingly?
- *If Jesus really was God then the answer is yes. He could have said a word and had the whole world that He created stop living around Him. He could have called the armies of Heaven to rescue Him, but He didn't. He could have defended Himself in front of Pilate, but He said nothing. He willingly sacrificed His life.*

Justified

Romans 5:6-11
⁶ For while we were still weak, at the right time Christ died for the ungodly. ⁷ For one will scarcely die for a righteous person—though perhaps for a good person one would dare even to die— ⁸ but God shows his love for us in that while we were still sinners, Christ died for us. ⁹ Since, therefore, we have now been justified by his blood, much more shall we be saved by him from the wrath of God. ¹⁰ For if while we were enemies we were reconciled to God by the death of his Son, much more, now that we are reconciled, shall we be saved by his life. ¹¹ More than that, we also rejoice in God through our Lord Jesus Christ, through whom we have now received reconciliation.

Recap *When we were weak in sin, Jesus died for us. This is God's love for us: that even when we were enemies with God, living in our selfishness, sin and pride, Jesus died for us. Now we are justified by His blood and saved from the wrath of God. Jesus reconciled us to God by His death and saves us through His life. It's a real reason to celebrate.*

Q: Why did Jesus die for us?
- To justify us by His blood and save us from the wrath of God. He died to reconcile us to God.

Q: What does justify mean?
- Justified is a legal term, meaning to declare righteous. It means that by Jesus' sacrifice we are declared righteous before God. Because we are righteous before God, we are no longer under His wrath, because God's wrath is only towards unrighteousness. All our sin and unrighteousness is taken away by Jesus, which means that we are now approved by God, not because of what we have done, but because of what Jesus has done for us.

Q: What does it mean to be reconciled to God?
- The unity is restored. We can live in unity with Him and come back into His image and design.

Q: What does the sacrifice of Jesus mean for the debt that we owe God?
- The wages of sin is death, in other words, sin demands death. Jesus died to take away our sin. The debt is removed.

Not Guilty

Romans 8:1-8
¹ There is therefore now no condemnation for those who are in Christ Jesus. ² For the law of the Spirit of life has set you free in Christ Jesus from the law of sin and death. ³

For God has done what the law, weakened by the flesh, could not do. By sending his own Son in the likeness of sinful flesh and for sin, he condemned sin in the flesh, [4] in order that the righteous requirement of the law might be fulfilled in us, who walk not according to the flesh but according to the Spirit.

Recap *There is no condemnation for people who are in Jesus. We are set free from sin and death by a law of the Spirit of life. The law couldn't save us, so Jesus came in the likeness of sinful flesh and condemned sin so that we might be righteous.*

> This can be a bit of a tricky passage to understand at first. The term "law" here refers to the standard of behavior that defines what it means to be righteous. It tells us which actions are good and which are evil. Just like the law of gravity describes the force that pulls us towards the earth, the moral law also describes the reality that *all sin leads to death.* It is inevitable. According to God's moral law, death is the inescapable consequence of sin, and it is as sure as any of His natural laws. The outcome is certain.
>
> But simply knowing that sin leads to death and having a set of rules and commands that define righteous behavior doesn't actually help us to overcome our sin or selfishness. It simply tells us that we are sinners and that we are going to die apart from God. So instead of helping us, knowing all the rules just leaves us feeling overwhelmed and helpless to live righteously before God.
>
> Condemnation is a death sentence. As long as we live in sin, we are living under a death sentence of separation from God. But, recognizing our helplessness, God sent Jesus to come as a person and to take our sin and die. Through His death, Jesus satisfied the law which stated that all sin must lead to death. He fulfilled the law and in doing so, He condemned sin itself. He died for us so that we won't be separated from God, now or ever for all eternity. He died to bring us back into unity with God. This is why there is no condemnation for those who are in Christ Jesus. There can't possibly be any condemnation for believers in Jesus because He has already died for our sin. Our sentence has already been served. The judgment has been already passed and executed through the sacrifice of Jesus Christ.

2 Corinthians 5:17-21
¹⁷ Therefore, if anyone is in Christ, he is a new creation. The old has passed away; behold, the new has come. ¹⁸ All this is from God, who through Christ reconciled us to himself and gave us the ministry of reconciliation; ¹⁹ that is, in Christ God was reconciling the world to himself, not counting their trespasses against them, and entrusting to us the message of reconciliation. ²⁰ Therefore, we are ambassadors for Christ, God making his appeal through us. We implore you on behalf of Christ, be reconciled to God. ²¹ For our sake he made him to be sin who knew no sin, so that in him we might become the righteousness of God.

Recap *If we are "in Christ" the old is gone and we are a new creation. God restored us to himself and didn't count our sin against us. Now He has given us this message to share with others. It was for our sake that God made Jesus (who never sinned) to be sin for us. Now in Christ we can live in the righteousness of God.*

Q: What is the message of reconciliation?
- *It is the message of a restored relationship with God through Jesus. When we receive His reconciliation it becomes our job to share this message with other people so they can also be restored in their relationship with God.*

Q: What does it mean that Jesus became sin?
- *All of our sin was placed on Him. The reality of Jesus 'becoming sin' was such that the serpent, which was typically a symbol for Satan, became a symbol for Jesus at His death (see John 3:14-16).*

Q: So if Jesus became sin for us, what happened to our sin when Jesus died?
- *It died with Him. All the actions of selfishness, lust, greed, and pride, they all died and were wiped out of history. Now we can be free to live in righteousness before God. This is why we can be justified before God, because Jesus took all our sin away.*
- *How can an action die? Our actions live through their consequences. When we act in love, the action can have resonating or cascading effects for years afterwards. Likewise, when we sin, our actions have devastating effects,*

both inwardly and outwardly. When our sin dies at the cross, all the spiritual effects of that sin, the separation from God, the guilt, pain and weight of that sin, it is all taken away. The sin dies.

Prophecy of the Lamb (if time allows)

" Around 700 years before Jesus came, God spoke to a prophet called Isaiah about Jesus. He had already revealed Jesus' birth to Isaiah. Now God spoke of His sacrificial death.

Isaiah 53
Who has believed what he has heard from us?
    And to whom has the arm of the Lord been revealed?
2 For he grew up before him like a young plant,
    and like a root out of dry ground;
    he had no form or majesty that we should look at him,
    and no beauty that we should desire him.
3 He was despised and rejected by men;
    a man of sorrows, and acquainted with grief;
    and as one from whom men hide their faces
    he was despised, and we esteemed him not.
4 Surely he has borne our griefs
    and carried our sorrows;
    yet we esteemed him stricken,
    smitten by God, and afflicted.
5 But he was pierced for our transgressions;
    he was crushed for our iniquities;
    upon him was the chastisement that brought us peace,
    and with his wounds we are healed.
6 All we like sheep have gone astray;
    we have turned—every one—to his own way;
    and the Lord has laid on him
    the iniquity of us all.

⁷ He was oppressed, and he was afflicted,
   yet he opened not his mouth;
   like a lamb that is led to the slaughter,
   and like a sheep that before its shearers is silent,
   so he opened not his mouth.
⁸ By oppression and judgment he was taken away;
   and as for his generation, who considered
   that he was cut off out of the land of the living,
   stricken for the transgression of my people?
⁹ And they made his grave with the wicked
   and with a rich man in his death,
   although he had done no violence,
   and there was no deceit in his mouth.
¹⁰ Yet it was the will of the Lord to crush him;
   he has put him to grief;
   when his soul makes an offering for guilt,
   he shall see his offspring; he shall prolong his days;
   the will of the Lord shall prosper in his hand.
¹¹ Out of the anguish of his soul he shall see and be satisfied;
   by his knowledge shall the righteous one, my servant,
   make many to be accounted righteous,
   and he shall bear their iniquities.
¹² Therefore I will divide him a portion with the many,
   and he shall divide the spoil with the strong,
   because he poured out his soul to death
   and was numbered with the transgressors;
   yet he bore the sin of many,
   and makes intercession for the transgressors.

Q: What insights does the prophecy give us into the death of Jesus?
- *Jesus was rejected and despised.*
- *He was pierced with nails on the cross and a spear in his side, see John 19:30-35, in order to pay the debt of our sin.*

- *All of us have gone astray and need Jesus to take away our sin.*
- *Jesus was perfectly innocent of sin, which uniquely qualified him to take away our sin.*
- *Jesus went through agony of soul and body.*
- *It was the will of God to crush Jesus and make him an offering for sin. God was the architect and orchestrator of the crucifixion. And it was all for love (see John 3:16, 1 John 4:10).*

Summary

God created us in His image, through Jesus and for Him. But like wandering sheep, we all went astray. We chose the way of selfishness and sin and strayed from our identity and purpose in life. We stole our lives away from Jesus. And in doing so, we took on a debt that was impossible to pay.

But the God of love had a plan for our redemption. He sent His Son Jesus, who was and is God, to be the sacrifice for our sins. Jesus was entirely innocent of all sin. He had done no violence, and was not selfish or sinful in any way. This made Him the only one who could possibly act as a sacrifice for sin. So Jesus took our punishment. He became sin for us. He was falsely accused, unjustly condemned, and cruelly crucified. He suffered a painful and humiliating execution, which is what our sin demands. Through His death, our sin was completely taken away. His sacrifice took away our corruption and completely paid our life-debt to God. In Christ we can be forever free from the bondage of sin and restored back into relationship with God.

8 | Home Reading and Questions

☐ **Matthew 27:11-54**

I: Imagine being in the court, listening to Pilate talking to Jesus. Imagine seeing His trial. Imagine watching Him being beaten, mocked and finally crucified. Imagine seeing Jesus on the cross, watching Him bleed. Imagine hearing Jesus cry out. Imagine Him looking at you before closing His eyes and dying.

Q: Did Jesus sound like He was sane when He talked with Pilate?

Q: Why did Pilate find no guilt in Jesus?

Q: Why did Jesus choose to suffer such humiliation and pain?

Q: Did Jesus really die for me? If not, why else would He choose to die? If so, what does that mean for me?

☐ **Psalm 22:1-24**
This Psalm was written by King David of Israel around 1000 years before Jesus' crucifixion.

I: Imagine the intensity of feeling as Jesus' life was poured out like water.

Q: How does this Psalm parallel Jesus' crucifixion?

Q: What emotion must Jesus have felt at the cross?

Q: Did God come through and deliver Him?

☐ **John 10:1-18**
Q: What is a good shepherd like?

Q: Did Jesus lay down His life at the cross willingly?

Q: Why?

☐ **Psalm 23**
Q: What does God promise me through this Psalm?

Q: What would it be like to know that I will never lack anything I need?

Q: What would it feel like for God to restore my soul?

Q: What would it be like to have goodness and love following me wherever I go?

☐ **Prayer** Jesus, did you really die for my sin? If so, why? Why would you die for me? Please show me what happened on the cross and how it can change my life.

☐ John 21 – Acts 1
Write down your questions here:

☐ Experiences with God
Write down some of your own prayers, discoveries, questions and experiences.

9 | Resurrection Life

Leader's Notes
This study looks more at how Jesus became the sacrifice to take away sin.

Key Goals
- *To show how Jesus took away sin at the cross, securing our forgiveness forever.*

The story of God's redemption doesn't end with the death of Jesus. Dying for our sin was only half the solution. In order for Jesus to complete His mission, He had to defeat both sin *and* death. So let's see how He does it.

Mark 8:27-31
²⁷ And Jesus went on with his disciples to the villages of Caesarea Philippi. And on the way he asked his disciples, "Who do people say that I am?" ²⁸ And they told him, "John the Baptist; and others say, Elijah; and others, one of the prophets." ²⁹ And he asked them, "But who do you say that I am?" Peter answered him, "You are the Christ." ³⁰ And he strictly charged them to tell no one about him.

³¹ And he began to teach them that the Son of Man must suffer many things and be rejected by the elders and the chief priests and the scribes and be killed, and after three days rise again.

Recap *Jesus asks his disciples who people are saying He is. They told Him. He asked them who they say He is. Peter said "the Christ". Jesus then taught them that He must suffer, be rejected and killed, and then rise again after three days.*

Q: Why would Jesus teach that He was going to suffer and die and rise again?
- *To prepare His disciples for what was coming and help them to look beyond His death.*

Matthew 27:57-28:20 (it's a long passage, so share the reading around the group)
⁵⁷ When it was evening, there came a rich man from Arimathea, named Joseph, who also was a disciple of Jesus. ⁵⁸ He went to Pilate and asked for the body of Jesus. Then Pilate ordered it to be given to him. ⁵⁹ And Joseph took the body and wrapped it in a clean linen shroud ⁶⁰ and laid it in his own new tomb, which he had cut in the rock. And he rolled a great stone to the entrance of the tomb and went away. ⁶¹ Mary Magdalene and the other Mary were there, sitting opposite the tomb.

⁶² The next day, that is, after the day of Preparation, the chief priests and the Pharisees gathered before Pilate ⁶³ and said, "Sir, we remember how that impostor said, while he was still alive, 'After three days I will rise.' ⁶⁴ Therefore order the tomb to be made secure until the third day, lest his disciples go and steal him away and tell the people, 'He has risen from the dead,' and the last fraud will be worse than the first." ⁶⁵ Pilate said to them, "You have a guard of soldiers. Go, make it as secure as you can." ⁶⁶ So they went and made the tomb secure by sealing the stone and setting a guard.

²⁸:¹ Now after the Sabbath, toward the dawn of the first day of the week, Mary Magdalene and the other Mary went to see the tomb. ² And behold, there was a great earthquake, for an angel of the Lord descended from heaven and came and rolled back the stone and sat on it. ³ His appearance was like lightning, and his clothing white as snow. ⁴ And for fear of him the guards trembled and became like dead men. ⁵ But the angel said to the women, "Do not be afraid, for I know that you seek Jesus who was crucified. ⁶ He is not here, for he has risen, as he said. Come, see the place where he lay. ⁷ Then go quickly and tell his disciples that he has risen from the dead, and behold, he is going before you to Galilee; there you will see him. See, I have told you." ⁸ So they departed quickly from the tomb with fear and great joy, and ran to tell his disciples. ⁹ And behold, Jesus met them and said, "Greetings!" And they came up and took hold of his feet and worshiped him. ¹⁰ Then Jesus said to them, "Do not be afraid; go and tell my brothers to go to Galilee, and there they will see me."

¹¹ While they were going, behold, some of the guard went into the city and told the chief priests all that had taken place. ¹² And when they had assembled with the elders and taken counsel, they gave a sufficient sum of money to the soldiers ¹³ and said, "Tell people, 'His disciples came by night and stole him away while we were asleep.' ¹⁴ And if this comes to the governor's ears, we will satisfy him and keep you

out of trouble." ¹⁵ So they took the money and did as they were directed. And this story has been spread among the Jews to this day.

¹⁶ Now the eleven disciples went to Galilee, to the mountain to which Jesus had directed them. ¹⁷ And when they saw him they worshiped him, but some doubted. ¹⁸ And Jesus came and said to them, "All authority in heaven and on earth has been given to me. ¹⁹ Go therefore and make disciples of all nations, baptizing them in the name of the Father and of the Son and of the Holy Spirit, ²⁰ teaching them to observe all that I have commanded you. And behold, I am with you always, to the end of the age."

Recap *Jesus was buried in a tomb. It was guarded by some soldiers. Mary and Mary went to the tomb and saw an angel. He said that Jesus had risen as was predicted. They left, and then met Jesus. They worshipped Him as God. He sent them to the others. The Jewish elders paid the guards to lie about Jesus' resurrection. The disciples went to Galilee and saw Jesus. Jesus then sent them to make more disciples and promised to be with them.*

Q: Was Jesus really raised from the dead? How is that even possible?
- *Just get some thoughts.*

Q: Jesus said He would rise again after His execution (*Mark 8:31, Luke 9:22*). What would it mean if Jesus didn't actually rise again?
- *If it didn't happen then Jesus would be guilty of lying—of sinning against God. This would mean that nothing Jesus said could be trusted, and that He certainly wasn't God. It ultimately means that believing in Jesus is a waste of time.*

Q: Is it more likely that Jesus was raised from dead by the power of God, or that He faked His resurrection?
- *Get some responses. Then possibly explore these points:*
- *How did Jesus look to Mary? When Jesus appeared to Mary, He did not look like someone who had spent six hours on a cross and had a spear thrust towards his heart, and all this after having been beaten, abused and*

whipped. So He could not have fallen into a near-death coma state and then woken up with enough strength to open the sealed tomb and overcome the soldiers. He could not have then gone on to pretend that He was raised when His injuries would have been so clearly visible to everyone. His poor physical state would have prevented anyone from believing that he was truly raised from the dead.
- *Is it possible to survive being crucified? There is no record of anyone, ever, surviving being crucified. The Romans made sure of it. Crucifixion always resulted in a painful and certain death.*
- *What impression did He leave people with? When they saw Jesus raised from the dead, the disciples were transformed from men who were scared and in hiding, to people who boldly and publicly preached Jesus. They were willing to be imprisoned and to be beaten and ultimately killed for their belief in Jesus. They were eye-witnesses who were convinced that Jesus was raised from the dead.*
- *In fact, of the remaining 11 disciples, at least eight were killed for their belief that Jesus rose from the dead. They could have said that the resurrection was a lie and saved their own lives, but they could not deny what they knew to be true: Jesus really did die and come back to life.*
- *It is easier to believe that Jesus really was God and really did die and rise again from the dead, than it is to believe that he was just a man that was nearly killed, mistaken for dead, and who went on to fool everyone into believing he rose from the dead. That idea just doesn't stack up. It's not backed up by logic or evidence. It is wishful thinking—a vain attempt to avoid believing in the reality of the resurrection of Jesus.*

Q: Why is the resurrection important?
- *Because by being raised from the dead, Jesus conquered both sin <u>and</u> death.*
- *It means that we worship and follow a living God. All the leaders from all other religions are dead and buried. But Jesus is alive, forever.*
- *It means that when we believe in Jesus, we have the assurance of eternal life, because He lives forever.*

- *It means that physical death is not the end for us. We will rise again because Jesus has said He will raise us up and give us eternal life.*

Q: How important is it to believe in the resurrection if we want to follow Jesus?
- *Essential. It is the foundational belief of those who follow Jesus.*
- *Without resurrection there is no forgiveness of sin, no victory over death, and no new life in the image of God.*

Q: So what does it mean to experience the cross and the resurrection in our lives?
- *Get some ideas.*

Immersed into Death and Life

Romans 6:1-4
¹ What shall we say then? Are we to continue in sin that grace may abound? ² By no means! How can we who died to sin still live in it? ³ Do you not know that all of us who have been baptized into Christ Jesus were baptized into his death? ⁴ We were buried therefore with him by baptism into death, in order that, just as Christ was raised from the dead by the glory of the Father, we too might walk in newness of life.

Recap We should not sin because everyone who has been baptized (immersed) into Jesus has been baptized into His death. We died with Christ so that just as He was raised, we might walk in newness of life. (We'll look at baptism later).

Q: What does it mean to be baptized (immersed) into the death of Jesus?
- *It means to let the full power of the cross into our lives. It means to die to sin. It means to let Jesus take all the sin and corruption out of our heart. It means that everything that is not of God in our lives is put to death with Jesus.*

Q: What does it mean to walk in "newness of life"?
- *It means to live in unity with Jesus. It means to have His eternal life.*

- *It means to live in victory over sin and darkness.*

United with Christ

Romans 6:5-11
⁵ For if we have been united with him in a death like his, we shall certainly be united with him in a resurrection like his. ⁶ We know that our old self was crucified with him in order that the body of sin might be brought to nothing, so that we would no longer be enslaved to sin. ⁷ For one who has died has been set free from sin. ⁸ Now if we have died with Christ, we believe that we will also live with him. ⁹ We know that Christ, being raised from the dead, will never die again; death no longer has dominion over him. ¹⁰ For the death he died he died to sin, once for all, but the life he lives he lives to God. ¹¹ So you also must consider yourselves dead to sin and alive to God in Christ Jesus.

Recap *If we are united with Jesus in death we will definitely be united with Him in resurrection life. Our old self was crucified with Him so that we would no longer be enslaved to sin. If we died with Christ we will live with Him. Jesus will never, ever die again. He is stronger than death. So we need to continually understand that in Christ we are dead to sin and alive to God.*

Q: Is resurrection life something we can experience now or is it for later, after we physically die?
- *It is both. Through His resurrection we can live in "the newness of life" now, with the promise that like Jesus, God will bring us back to life after we physically die.*

Q: What does it mean for the "old self" to be crucified with Christ? What is the old self?
- *Just get some ideas.*

The Old Self

Colossians 3:1-11
¹ If then you have been raised with Christ, seek the things that are above, where Christ is, seated at the right hand of God. ² Set your minds on things that are above, not on things that are on earth. ³ For you have died, and your life is hidden with Christ in God. ⁴ When Christ who is your life appears, then you also will appear with him in glory.

⁵ Put to death therefore what is earthly in you: sexual immorality, impurity, passion, evil desire, and covetousness, which is idolatry. ⁶ On account of these the wrath of God is coming. ⁷ In these you too once walked, when you were living in them. ⁸ But now you must put them all away: anger, wrath, malice, slander, and obscene talk from your mouth. ⁹ Do not lie to one another, seeing that you have put off the old self with its practices ¹⁰ and have put on the new self, which is being renewed in knowledge after the image of its creator. ¹¹ Here there is not Greek and Jew, circumcised and uncircumcised, barbarian, Scythian, slave, free; but Christ is all, and in all.

Recap If we have been raised with Jesus, then we need to set our minds on things above. Our lives are hidden in God and we will appear with Jesus in glory. So we need to put to death every evil and selfish desire, because God's judgment is coming. We used to live like that, but now we have to get rid of all these ways and put off the old self. Now we need to put on our new self which is being renewed according to the image of God. So now there is no distinction between people, but Jesus is all and in all.

The "old self" is our old identity. It is the corrupt nature within our hearts that compels us to sin. It is all the darkness and selfishness within us that distorts God's image and design for our lives. In Scripture, the old self is also simply called *the flesh*.

The "new self" is our new identity in union with Jesus. It is who we truly are: people created in the image of God, who live in His love and power. Through the cross, Jesus released His power to bring the old self to death, and through His resurrection He released His power to bring us into the reality of our new identity in His image.

Q: What would it be like for the "old self" to be crucified with Christ?
- *Awesome. It would be like having everything bad being killed off.*

Q: How can this happen?
- *It is God's work to crucify our old-life, but we need to fully participate in His work in order to experience the reality. We need to actively respond to the cross and commit all our energies into putting off the old self—discarding it like an unwanted garment—and putting on the new self.*
- *Identity is the key here. If we make the old life a part of our identity, it will be impossible to truly put it off. In order to put off the old and put on the new, we need to keep on being renewed, growing every day in the true identity that Jesus created for us. We cannot afford to waste any time wavering between two different identities. The call of God is clear: we need to die to the old and embrace the new.*

Q: What would our new self look like? How would it feel?
- *It would look like a life of relentless, selfless love. It would look like a life of close connection with Jesus. We'll look at this more in the next study.*

Summary

Long before He died, Jesus told His disciples that it was essential that He suffer, die and rise again. The disciples didn't understand it at the time, but everything Jesus said came to pass. He was arrested, tortured, abused and humiliated. Because of His love, the Son of God, for whom all creation was made, willingly let Himself be hung on a cross, exposed, shamed and mocked by His own creation. Yet far from being a defeat, Jesus' unjust execution was all a part of God's plan to free us from all sin. The cross was a resounding victory. Sin was put to death.

Having conquered sin, Jesus then overcame death itself. The Spirit of God raised Him back to life and now Jesus lives forever and cannot ever die. Now he invites us to be united with Him in his death and resurrection. Jesus calls us to let Him crucify our old life so that we can experience a new life through the power of His resurrection.

9 | Home Reading and Questions

☐ **1 Corinthians 15:1-19**
Q: How many people did Jesus appear to after His resurrection?

Q: Why is Jesus' resurrection so important?

I: Imagine being among all the people who saw Jesus. Imagine that you watched Him die, and now you see Him alive. Imagine Him looking through the crowd and locking eyes with you.

☐ **1 Peter 2:21-25**
Q: Who did Jesus suffer for?

Q: Why did Jesus bear our sins on the cross?

Q: How are we healed by Jesus' wounds?

Q: Am I straying away, or am I returning to the Shepherd and Guardian of my soul?

☐ **Philippians 3:7-11**
Q: What would it be like to know the power of Jesus' resurrection?

Q: What would it be like to be conformed to His death?

Q: Do I want my old life to be crucified with Jesus?

Q: Do I want a new life with Jesus?

Q: What would my new life with Jesus look like?

☐ **Prayer** Jesus, if you're alive now, please help me to believe. Help me to really believe that you died and rose again, so that I could die with you and rise with you. Help me to really want this.

☐ **Acts 2-3**
Write down your questions here:

☐ Experiences with God
Write down some of your own prayers, discoveries, questions and experiences.

10 | Grace through Faith

Leader's Notes
This study looks more at how we can receive the forgiveness of God in our lives.

Key Goals
- To show how God's forgiveness is total and His blood washes away all sin.
- To show what it means to have faith in Jesus.
- To look at what it means to repent from our sin.

Jesus died and was raised again for us. He died to take away our sin, and He was raised again so that we might have eternal life—an unending life in His image, in union with Him. In this study we will look at how we receive this new life.

Acts 2:22-41 (can skip ahead to verse 36 if you like)
²² "Men of Israel, hear these words: Jesus of Nazareth, a man attested to you by God with mighty works and wonders and signs that God did through him in your midst, as you yourselves know— ²³ this Jesus, delivered up according to the definite plan and foreknowledge of God, you crucified and killed by the hands of lawless men. ²⁴ God raised him up, loosing the pangs of death, because it was not possible for him to be held by it. ²⁵ For David says concerning him,

> "'I saw the Lord always before me,
> for he is at my right hand that I may not be shaken;
> ²⁶ therefore my heart was glad, and my tongue rejoiced;
> my flesh also will dwell in hope.
> ²⁷ For you will not abandon my soul to Hades,
> or let your Holy One see corruption.
> ²⁸ You have made known to me the paths of life;
> you will make me full of gladness with your presence.'

| 105

²⁹ "Brothers, I may say to you with confidence about the patriarch David that he both died and was buried, and his tomb is with us to this day. ³⁰ Being therefore a prophet, and knowing that God had sworn with an oath to him that he would set one of his descendants on his throne, ³¹ he foresaw and spoke about the resurrection of the Christ, that he was not abandoned to Hades, nor did his flesh see corruption. ³² This Jesus God raised up, and of that we all are witnesses. ³³ Being therefore exalted at the right hand of God, and having received from the Father the promise of the Holy Spirit, he has poured out this that you yourselves are seeing and hearing. ³⁴ For David did not ascend into the heavens, but he himself says,

> "'The Lord said to my Lord,
> "Sit at my right hand,
> ³⁵ until I make your enemies your footstool."'

³⁶ Let all the house of Israel therefore know for certain that God has made him both Lord and Christ, this Jesus whom you crucified."

³⁷ Now when they heard this they were cut to the heart, and said to Peter and the rest of the apostles, "Brothers, what shall we do?" ³⁸ And Peter said to them, "Repent and be baptized every one of you in the name of Jesus Christ for the forgiveness of your sins, and you will receive the gift of the Holy Spirit. ³⁹ For the promise is for you and for your children and for all who are far off, everyone whom the Lord our God calls to himself." ⁴⁰ And with many other words he bore witness and continued to exhort them, saying, "Save yourselves from this crooked generation." ⁴¹ So those who received his word were baptized, and there were added that day about three thousand souls.

Recap *God did awesome signs through Jesus. He was killed and then raised up by God. David spoke of it (around 1000 years earlier) saying that Jesus would not see corruption or stay dead. Jesus is now raised up and exalted to be back with God and He has poured out His Spirit. So Jesus is Lord and Christ. When the people heard it, they were cut to the heart and wanted to respond. Peter called them to repent and be baptized for the forgiveness of sins, because the promise is for everyone. 3000 people believed that day.*

Q: What does it mean to repent for the forgiveness of sins?
- *In the Old Testament Hebrew, repentance means changing direction and returning to God. Like the prodigal (wayward/rebellious) son we need to return to God. We need to leave our old ways and come to God.*
- *In the New Testament, the word "repent" means to change our mind or alter the way we think. Repentance calls for a change of heart and mind, leading to a change of action.*
- *If we are to come to Jesus, we need to be willing to let Him change us.*

" In terms of receiving the power of the cross, we repent when we turn to God and seek Him to crucify our old life. We repent when we disown our old identity and seek God for His image. Repentance is giving up on going our own way in life and seeking God to show us His way. If we repent and turn to God, our forgiveness is guaranteed. God will completely forgive every wrong, every sin, and every act of selfishness forever. Our spiritual state will be totally clean and we will be completely innocent before God.

Baptism

Q: Why did the people get baptized when they believed?
- *Just get ideas.*

" Water baptism is an expression of faith and repentance. It is a sign that we believe God and that we have given our lives back to Him. When we get baptized in water, we make the statement that we are uniting ourselves with Jesus, and we are living for Him. We are giving our old life over to be crucified with Him, and we are receiving His gift of new life. Without faith, being immersed or baptized in water achieves nothing. But with faith, it becomes a powerful expression of our new life with Jesus.

When people fall in love and commit to sharing the rest or their lives with each other, they get married. They publically declare their love and invite their friends to their wedding to celebrate their new life together. In many ways, baptism is like the wedding celebration. It is a public declaration of our love for God and a chance for others to celebrate our new life with us.

Forgiveness through the Blood

1 John 1:5-10
⁵ This is the message we have heard from him and proclaim to you, that God is light, and in him is no darkness at all. ⁶ If we say we have fellowship with him while we walk in darkness, we lie and do not practice the truth. ⁷ But if we walk in the light, as he is in the light, we have fellowship with one another, and the blood of Jesus his Son cleanses us from all sin. ⁸ If we say we have no sin, we deceive ourselves, and the truth is not in us. ⁹ If we confess our sins, he is faithful and just to forgive us our sins and to cleanse us from all unrighteousness. ¹⁰ If we say we have not sinned, we make him a liar, and his word is not in us.

Recap *God is light and so we cannot have fellowship with Him and still live in darkness. We need to come into His light and let Jesus' blood cleanse us from all sin. If we say that we have no sin, we are deceived. But if we admit our sin and our need for Jesus, then He will forgive all our sins and cleanse us from all unrighteousness.*

Q: Do we really need Jesus to cleanse us from our sin?

- *Yes. We cannot be clean apart from His blood. All other religions try to buy their own redemption through good works, meditation, secret knowledge and rituals, or by self-denial. Some religions pretend that there is no such thing as good and evil, that sin is an illusion and so there is no need for a savior. But God is clear: sin is real. The design of God is real. The fallen, sinful corruption of His humanity is real. So God sent Jesus to be the one and only and final solution for sin. He came as a real man. He died a real death. And our need for Him is more real than we can possibly comprehend.*
- *There is no forgiveness of sin apart from the blood of Jesus. He is the only way.*

Q: What does it mean to confess our sins?
- *The Greek word for "confess" means to agree or come to the same conclusion. So when we confess our sins, we agree with God that we have lived in sin and that we need Jesus to cleanse us.*
- *The next step of confession is to agree with God about the power of His blood to wash away our sin and make us truly clean. It is to agree with His word and truly believe that we are completely innocent in His eyes, because Jesus has taken all our sin away.*

Q: What does it mean to be cleansed from all sin? What would that feel like?
- *Sin bears a weight of condemnation over a person. To be forgiven of all our sin and reunited with God is like having an immense weight removed. It's like getting a new life, being born again. All the guilt is washed away. Someone in the group may have a testimony of what it felt like to receive the forgiveness of God through Jesus.*

Removing Sin

Psalm 103:11-13
¹¹ For as high as the heavens are above the earth,
  so great is his steadfast love toward those who fear him;
¹² as far as the east is from the west,
  so far does he remove our transgressions (sins) from us.
¹³ As a father shows compassion to his children,
  so the Lord shows compassion to those who fear him.

Recap *God's love towards us is greater than we can imagine. His forgiveness is more complete than we could imagine. He is compassionate to us like a loving parent.*

Q: How far does God remove our sin from us?
- *When Jesus takes our sin away, He removes it completely. "As far as the east is from the west" is a metaphor for an infinite distance. His was an infinite atonement. In effect, in God's eyes, it becomes as if we had never sinned at all.*

Jeremiah 31:33-34

^{33} For this is the covenant that I will make with the house of Israel after those days, declares the Lord: I will put my law within them, and I will write it on their hearts. And I will be their God, and they shall be my people. ^{34} And no longer shall each one teach his neighbor and each his brother, saying, 'Know the Lord,' for they shall all know me, from the least of them to the greatest, declares the Lord. For I will forgive their iniquity, and I will remember their sin no more."

Recap *God will make a new covenant with Israel. He'll put their laws in their hearts and be their God. Everyone will know God because He will forgive their iniquity and forget their sin.*

Q: How is it possible for God to forget our sin?
- *If it has been washed away by the blood of Jesus then it has died. It has been destroyed out of all existence. Even if we can remember our sin, God does not. He will never, ever condemn us for our sin or hold it against us, because Jesus has suffered the full wrath and judgment of God upon sin. In God's eyes, we are innocent and clean. There is simply no more anger left for us.*

Q: If God cleanses our hearts and forgets our sin, how does that affect our identity?
- *We need to see ourselves as innocent before God. We need to let go of our old identity and embrace His design for our lives, as redeemed and restored people.*

By Grace, Through Faith

Ephesians 2:8-10
⁸ For by grace you have been saved through faith. And this is not your own doing; it is the gift of God, ⁹ not a result of works, so that no one may boast. ¹⁰ For we are his workmanship, created in Christ Jesus for good works, which God prepared beforehand, that we should walk in them.

Recap *We've been saved by grace, through faith. And that's not our own doing: it is the gift of God. He created us in Christ Jesus for good works.*

Romans 5:1-2
¹ Therefore, since we have been justified by faith, we have peace with God through our Lord Jesus Christ. ² Through him we have also obtained access by faith into this grace in which we stand, and we rejoice in hope of the glory of God.

Recap *We have been justified by faith and have peace with God through Jesus. We have obtained access by faith into God's grace, and we celebrate in the hope of His glory.*

Q: What is grace?
- *Grace is God's unearned and undeserved power and blessing.*
- *Salvation, and the inheritance it brings with it, is a gift of God's grace. It is not a right or a reward. It is not something we can earn. It makes no sense to try and earn a gift, because if we have earned it through good works then it is no longer a gift at all. Instead it becomes something that we can take credit for earning. But salvation is not like that. The price of redemption is too high for anyone to possibly earn. It was God's love that sent Jesus to die. It was God's love that took our sin. It is God's love that redeems us. Salvation is entirely a work of God's grace and love.*
- *So our only part in salvation is to open our hearts and receive the free gift. All we can do is be confident in the Giver, knowing that He has offered it to us, the offer stands, and all we have to do is receive it from Him.*

Q: How can we access the grace of God?
- *Through faith. Faith is the only way to receive grace.*

Q: So what is faith?
- *Just get ideas.*

> In Scripture, the Greek word translated as *faith* means to be persuaded or to be convinced. In simple terms, faith is being confident in our hearts that what God says is really true.

Faith of the Heart

Romans 10:8-10
⁸ But what does it say? "The word is near you, in your mouth and in your heart" (that is, the word of faith that we proclaim); ⁹ because, if you confess with your mouth that Jesus is Lord and believe in your heart that God raised him from the dead, you will be saved. ¹⁰ For with the heart one believes and is justified, and with the mouth one confesses and is saved.

Recap *The word is in our heart. If we say that Jesus is Lord (meaning God) and believe in our hearts Jesus was raised from the dead then we will be saved. We believe with our hearts, and confess with our mouths.*

Q: What does it mean to believe with our hearts?
- *To believe at the deepest level, with our entire being.*

Q: What does this say about intellectual belief?
- *Intellectual belief is not enough. We cannot be saved simply by agreeing with the teachings of the Bible. We need to believe with our whole being. We need to invest ourselves in the belief that God is real and Jesus really did die and rise for us.*

Q: How can we tell the difference between head-knowledge (intellectual belief) and heart-knowledge (faith)?
- *Just get ideas...*

Q: How do we get genuine faith? How do we get true heart-knowledge?
- *Faith is a gift from God. We cannot manufacture a deep confidence in God. We cannot persuade ourselves that He is real. All we can do is decide to believe and then cry out to God to create real faith in our hearts. And He will. God is good and does good. He will never withhold anything good from us when we cry out to Him. If we ask for faith in Jesus, He will give it to us.*

Summary

"To be saved from our sin is a gift of God's love. There is nothing we can do to earn it. We simply believe—truly believe. We receive faith and confidence from God, and just enjoy the reality of being forgiven through Jesus and set free from sin.

When we believe something in our heart, our lives change. The way we think about God, ourselves, and the world around us, all changes. Our actions change. This change is called repentance. It is dying to our old life and living with Jesus. When we believe in Jesus and are prepared to turn from our old life, we can express our faith through baptism. Through baptism we publicly declare that we have joined our lives to Jesus and we will be united with Him in death and in life. Our new life has begun and it's a cause for celebration!

10 | Home Reading and Questions

☐ **Hebrews 4:1-3**
I: Imagine what it would be like to experience spiritual rest—the end of stress and striving, and instead having a sense of continual peace.

Q: Has God given me a promise of entering into rest?

Q: What does it mean to come short of the promise?

Q: How can I hear the word of God and have faith?

Q: Do I want to receive the gift of faith?

☐ **Hebrews 12:1-2**
Q: Why did Jesus endure the cross?

Q: What was the joy set before Him?

Q: Could Jesus find joy in me?

Q: What does it mean for Jesus to be the author of my faith?

Q: What does it mean for Jesus to be the perfecter of my faith?

☐ **Romans 1:16-17**
Q: How is the gospel the power of salvation?

Q: What would it mean for me to live by faith?

☐ **Acts 3:17-21**
Q: What does it me for me to "repent and return"?

Q: Can't I just believe and be forgiven without needing to repent?

Q: What would it be like to be refreshed in the presence of God?

☐ **Acts 4-5**
Write down your questions here:

☐ Experiences with God
Write down some of your own prayers, discoveries, questions and experiences.

11 | Born Again

Leader's Notes

This study looks closer at what it means to be born again.

Key Goals
- To show how God's forgiveness is total and His blood washes away all sin.
- To show what it means to have faith in Jesus.
- To look at what it means to repent from our sin.

Born Again

John 3:3-8

³ Now there was a man of the Pharisees named Nicodemus, a ruler of the Jews. ² This man came to Jesus by night and said to him, "Rabbi, we know that you are a teacher come from God, for no one can do these signs that you do unless God is with him." ³ Jesus answered him, "Truly, truly, I say to you, unless one is born again he cannot see the kingdom of God." ⁴ Nicodemus said to him, "How can a man be born when he is old? Can he enter a second time into his mother's womb and be born?" ⁵ Jesus answered, "Truly, truly, I say to you, unless one is born of water and the Spirit, he cannot enter the kingdom of God. ⁶ That which is born of the flesh is flesh, and that which is born of the Spirit is spirit. ⁷ Do not marvel that I said to you, 'You must be born again.' ⁸ The wind blows where it wishes, and you hear its sound, but you do not know where it comes from or where it goes. So it is with everyone who is born of the Spirit."

Recap *Nicodemus comes to Jesus and says that He is from God because of all the miracles. Jesus says that a person has to be born again to see the kingdom of God.*

Nicodemus thinks this is physically impossible. Jesus says that we need to be born of water and Spirit in order to enter into the kingdom of God. The Spirit is like wind and goes where it likes, so it is with people who are born of the Spirit.

Q: What does it mean to be born of water?
- *Being baptized in water is like a new life experience. It is a sign of our faith in Jesus and our new life in Him.*

Q: What does it mean to be born of the Spirit?
- *To find new life in the Spirit of God.*

John 1:29-33 (John the Baptist speaking)
[29] The next day he saw Jesus coming toward him, and said, "Behold, the Lamb of God, who takes away the sin of the world! [30] This is he of whom I said, 'After me comes a man who ranks before me, because he was before me.' [31] I myself did not know him, but for this purpose I came baptizing with water, that he might be revealed to Israel." [32] And John bore witness: "I saw the Spirit descend from heaven like a dove, and it remained on him. [33] I myself did not know him, but he who sent me to baptize with water said to me, 'He on whom you see the Spirit descend and remain, this is he who baptizes with the Holy Spirit.'

Recap *John called Jesus the Lamb who takes the sin of the world. John baptized people in water to prepare them for Jesus. When Jesus was baptized by John, the Spirit descended and rested on Him. That was a sign that Jesus was the One who would baptize or immerse people in the Holy Spirit.*

Q: *Baptize* is a Greek word meaning *immerse.* What does it mean to be immersed in the Spirit of Jesus?
- *It means to let the Spirit of Jesus saturate us—to get into every part of who we are. It is more than just a single experience of the Spirit, it is an ongoing union.*

- *In ancient times, a garment could be dipped in dye, but it was only baptized when the dye had saturated the garment and the dye was no longer separable from the material. Through baptism the garment was permanently changed and the result was a new united product: a dyed garment. So it is with the Spirit, when we are baptized in the Spirit we are a new creation, a person inseparably filled with Spirit of God.*

Q: What would it mean for our hearts to be soaked through with the Spirit of Jesus?
- *Encourage people to imagine the Spirit of Jesus, soaking and saturating every part of them.*
- *We would be continually changed at the core of our being. It's like our hearts would soak in His love and merge with the heart of Jesus. 2 Peter 1:4 calls this partaking of the divine nature. The more we receive of His Spirit, the more we share His heart—His feelings, His motives, His intentions, and His thoughts. This is not to say that every thought we have will be from God—on the contrary we need to test our thoughts because lots of thoughts won't actually reflect Jesus' heart. But lots will. As we grow in God, we will become more and more aware of which thoughts and feelings (or intuitions) are of the Spirit of Jesus and which are not.*

Q: How do we get immersed in the Spirit?
- *We simply open our hearts and ask Jesus to fill us with His Spirit.*

The Image of God

Romans 8:28-30
[28] And we know that for those who love God all things work together for good, for those who are called according to his purpose. [29] For those whom he foreknew he also predestined to be conformed to the image of his Son, in order that he might be the firstborn among many brothers. [30] And those whom he predestined he also called, and those whom he called he also justified, and those whom he justified he also glorified.

Recap *God makes everything work for good for those who are called. Those that he foreknew he destined to be conformed to the image of his Son. And those who were pre-destined, he has called, justified and glorified.*

> The Greek word *proorizo* translated as *predestined* has the sense of designing or defining a plan. Unlike the English word *predestined, proorizo* is not limited to a future destiny, but it also speaks of a present experience. Being conformed to the image of Jesus is something that we can experience now, in this life.

Q: What does it mean to conform something?
- It means to change something to be the same as something else.

Q: What does it mean to be conformed to the image of Jesus?
- It means to be brought into unity with Jesus so that we share His image.
- It means to be transformed inwardly so that we share our heart, soul and mind with Jesus.
- It means to be filled with God's Spirit so that we become more and more like Jesus.

Q: What is the image of Jesus like?
- God is love (1 John 4:16) so Jesus is love. To be recreated in His image means that we are filled with the love of God. His love defines us.

Q: How are we conformed to the image of Jesus?
- We believe in Him. We give our lives to Him. We seek God, continually asking Him to transform us. We open our hearts to be filled with His Spirit.

2 Corinthians 3:17-18
[17] Now the Lord is the Spirit, and where the Spirit of the Lord is, there is freedom. [18] And we all, with unveiled face, beholding the glory of the Lord, are being transformed into the same image from one degree of glory to another. For this comes from the Lord who is the Spirit.

Recap *There is freedom wherever the Spirit of Jesus is. He has taken away the veils (that stopped us seeing His truth) and now as we look at the glory of Jesus we are transformed into His image, from one degree of glory to another. This is all from the Lord Jesus, who is the Spirit.*

Q: Who is the Spirit of God?
- *"Lord" here refers to Jesus. It is saying that the Holy Spirit is the Spirit of Jesus. They are One. See Philippians 1:19 which refers to the Holy Spirit as "the Spirit of Jesus Christ".*

Q: What does it mean to be transformed?
- *Get some ideas.*
- *The Greek word metamorphoo (like metamorphosis in English) means: meta—"change after being with" and morphoo—"form in keeping with inner reality". So literally it means to be "transformed inwardly after being with…" When we spend time with Jesus, we are changed. We become like him.*
- *The transformation works from the inside out. As we spend time with Jesus, our inner reality is changed. Our heart, soul and mind are all changed to reflect the love of Jesus Christ.*

Q: What does it mean: from glory to glory?
- *Change is ongoing. We continually become more and more like Jesus. And every stage is glorious.*

Q: So how does it all happen? How are we transformed by the Spirit of Jesus?
- *Just get ideas.*

Regeneration

Titus 3:4-7
⁴ But when the goodness and loving kindness of God our Savior appeared, ⁵ he saved us, not because of works done by us in righteousness, but according to his own mercy, by the washing of regeneration and renewal of the Holy Spirit, ⁶ whom he poured out on us richly through Jesus Christ our Savior, ⁷ so that being justified by his grace we might become heirs according to the hope of eternal life.

Recap *When the kindness of God appeared, He saved us because of His mercy, by regenerating and renewing us in His Spirit so that we might becomes heirs of eternal life.*

Q: What is regeneration?
- *The Greek word palig-genesis which literally means new/again - birth/origin/creation. The Holy Spirit makes us a new creation in the image of Jesus.*
- *The Holy Spirit is the Spirit of Jesus, so when receive the Holy Spirit we are again united with Jesus and share His image.*

Summary

" If we are to follow Jesus, we need to be born again, in water and Spirit. We need to be prepared to let Jesus bring death to our old-self through the cross, and bring new life to us through His Spirit. We make a public statement of our choice to die with Christ to sin and to live in unity with Him when we are baptized in water. The baptism of water is a symbol of the end of the old life and the beginning of a new life in relationship with God.

When Jesus fills us with His Spirit, we receive the power to live in unity with Him—the power to love with His love, to work with His power, and to live in reality through His truth. With the Spirit we receive a new image for our lives, a new identity and design. This is the gift that Jesus offers us: a whole new life in relationship with Him. The gift has been given and it is our choice to receive it or not.

11 | Home Reading and Questions

☐ **Romans 8:31-37**
I: Imagine living a life saturated in the love of Jesus. Imagine that nothing could separate you from His love. Imagine going through the difficulties of life, even dangers and loss, but always having the love of Jesus with you. Imagine overwhelmingly overcoming every challenge in life, all through the love of Jesus.

Q: What would it feel like to know that God is for me?

Q: Does God really want to freely give me everything I need?

Q: What can separate me from the love of Jesus?

Q: How can I know more of God's love for me?

☐ **John 15:1-11**
I: Imagine a vine. Imagine the nutrients and life of the vine, flowing through to the branches. Imagine the fruit growing on the branches.

Q: What does it mean for me to be connected to Jesus?

Q: What does it mean for Jesus' words to abide in me?

Q: What would it be like to have the joy of Jesus in my heart?

☐ **John 15:12-17**
Q: How can I love other people like Jesus loves me?

Q: What does it mean for me to be a friend of God?

Q: Has Jesus chosen me?

Q: Have I chosen Jesus?

☐ **Acts 6-7**
Write down your questions here:

☐ Experiences with God
Write down some of your own prayers, discoveries, questions and experiences.

12 | A New Beginning

Leader's Notes
This study gives a look at the overall message of the course.

Key Goals
- To show that Jesus is the only way to God.
- To consider the cost of following Jesus.
- To invite people to make a decision to follow Jesus.

Eternal Life

John 3:16
For God so loved the world, that he gave his only Son, that whoever believes in him should not perish but have eternal life.

Recap *For God so loved the world, that he gave his only Son, that whoever believes in him should not perish but have eternal life.*

Q: What does it mean to believe in Jesus?
- *To have faith in Him. To believe in our hearts that He took away our sin when He died and that He rose again so that we could live with Him.*

❝ The original Greek wording for this passage says that whoever believes *into* Jesus should not perish but have eternal life *right now and into the* future (communicated through the Greek present tense). So eternal life starts as soon as we begin to believe into Jesus and continues for all eternity.

Q: What does it mean to believe *into* Jesus?
- *It means that through faith we are united with Jesus. To believe into Jesus means to share our lives with Him—to share our hearts, our souls and minds and all our resources with Him. It also means for Jesus to share Himself with us: to share His heart, His love, His blessings, and His power with us.*

Q: What is eternal life? What does it mean to have eternal life now?
- *It is living in union with Jesus. It is experiencing His life now and forever. See John 17:3 – "This is eternal life, that they may intimately and continually know you, the only true God, and Jesus Christ whom you have sent."*

The Only Way

John 14:6
Jesus said to him, "I am the way, and the truth, and the life. No one comes to the Father except through me."

Recap *Jesus is the way, and the truth, and the life. No one can possibly come to the Father except through Jesus.*

Q: Why is Jesus the only way to the Father?
- *Because He is God. He is one with the Father and so it's only through Jesus that we can know God. So Jesus is not a way to God. He is the only way.*
- *Only Jesus takes away the sin which separates us from God. There is no other way to deal with sin. The blood of Jesus is the only solution to sin.*
- *Jesus is the resurrection and the life (John 11:1-44). He overcame death itself. So when we believe in Jesus we are guaranteed resurrection life, even after we physically die. Only Jesus makes it all possible.*

Matthew 7:13-14

¹³ "Enter by the narrow gate. For the gate is wide and the way is easy that leads to destruction, and those who enter by it are many. ¹⁴ For the gate is narrow and the way is hard that leads to life, and those who find it are few.

Recap *It's easy to go our own way like everyone else, but in the end it leads us to death. It's hard to choose to follow Jesus, but He is the only way to life.*

Q: What does Jesus say about the way that leads to life?
- *That the way is hard and not many people truly follow the way.*

Q: Why is it hard to choose to follow Jesus?
- *Because there's a cost to it.*

Q: What is the cost of following Jesus?
- *We need to die to our old life and all selfishness. We need to give Him everything we are and everything we have. We need to be prepared to give up everything and let Him lead us.*

Counting the Cost

Mark 12:28-33

²⁸ And one of the scribes came up and heard them disputing with one another, and seeing that he answered them well, asked him, "Which commandment is the most important of all?" ²⁹ Jesus answered, "The most important is, 'Hear, O Israel: The Lord our God, the Lord is one. ³⁰ And you shall love the Lord your God with all your heart and with all your soul and with all your mind and with all your strength.' ³¹ The second is this: 'You shall love your neighbor as yourself.' There is no other commandment greater than these." ³² And the scribe said to him, "You are right, Teacher. You have truly said that he is one, and there is no other besides him. ³³ And to love him with all the heart and with all the understanding and with all the strength, and to love one's neighbor as oneself, is much more than all whole burnt offerings and sacrifices."

Recap *A man asks Jesus what matters most. He says that the most important command is to love God with everything we are, and love other people as if they were us. The man agrees. He says that loving God and loving others is more important than all the religious offerings.*

Q: What does this passage show us about following Jesus?
- *That we need to love Him with everything we are and love everyone around us.*
- *That love defines what it means to know and follow Jesus.*
- *That to live in the image of God is to always love.*

Q: Is there a cost to loving God and loving others?
- *Explore what love looks like and the cost to self.*
- *If self is dead then can there be a cost to self?*

Matthew 10:37-39

37 "Whoever loves father or mother more than me is not worthy of me, and whoever loves son or daughter more than me is not worthy of me. 38 And whoever does not take his cross and follow me is not worthy of me. 39 Whoever finds his life will lose it, and whoever loses his life for my sake will find it."

Recap *If we love anyone more than Jesus, we are not worthy of Him. If we are not prepared to take our cross and follow Jesus, we are not worthy. If we find our life we'll lose it. If we lose our life for Jesus, we will find it.*

Q: Why is it so important to love Jesus more than anyone or anything?
- *He is God. We've been made for Him. We need to put Him first in every way. He needs to come first in our relationships, in our work, in our free time. He needs to come before all our possessions. We are not our own (1 Corinthians 6:19-20) — everything we are and everything we have belongs to Jesus to do with as He likes.*

Q: What does it mean to lose our life if we find it and find it when we lose it?
- *If we are prepared to die to our old life then we'll find our true life with Jesus. But if we insist on holding onto our old life, we'll ultimately lose the life we are trying so hard to keep.*

John 15:17-20

[17] "These things I command you, so that you will love one another. [18] If the world hates you, know that it has hated me before it hated you. [19] If you were of the world, the world would love you as its own; but because you are not of the world, but I chose you out of the world, therefore the world hates you. [20] Remember the word that I said to you: 'A servant is not greater than his master.' If they persecuted me, they will also persecute you. If they kept my word, they will also keep yours."

Recap *We need to love each other. Some people in the world will hate us. They would love us if we were like them, but God has chosen us out of the world to be different, so worldly people will hate us. But they did the same to Jesus, and we are not better than Him, so it should come as no surprise if they give us a hard time.*

Q: What is the promise that is made in this passage?
- *If Jesus endured persecution then as followers of Jesus we can expect some degree of persecution in our lives.*
- *This is especially true in many countries around the world. For many people, when they decide to follow Jesus, their decisions can cost them their lives. For some it costs them their family and friends, their property and even their homeland.*

Q: What could be the cost for us?
- *Just get some ideas.*
- *Think of external costs: possible rejection, loss of relationship, possible injustice, loss of material possessions (giving to others in need) etc.*
- *Think of internal costs: loss of self, loss of control, the need for continual obedience etc.*

Q: What is the reward of following Jesus? What's the benefit?
- *Get some ideas.*
- *Eternal life. The love of God. Joy, peace, provision, security. Freedom. Forgiveness. The riches of God's blessing. The adventure of knowing God. A life in the image of God. The fulfillment of living in God's design. A sense of purpose. A sense of belonging. A sense of destiny.*

Q: So will it be worth the cost?
- *Yes. Yes it will. Regardless of the sacrifice, the choice to follow Jesus is always worth the cost. God's love never fails and He promises that the glory to come will be incomparable to any suffering we may endure in life.*
- *See Romans 8:16-18 – "The Spirit himself bears witness with our spirit that we are children of God, and if children, then heirs—heirs of God and fellow heirs with Christ, provided we suffer with him in order that we may also be glorified with him. For I consider that the sufferings of this present time are not worth comparing with the glory that is to be revealed to us."*

Day of Salvation

I Corinthians 5:14 – 6:10
[14] For the love of Christ controls us, because we have concluded this: that one has died for all, therefore all have died; [15] and he died for all, that those who live might no longer live for themselves but for him who for their sake died and was raised.

[16] From now on, therefore, we regard no one according to the flesh. Even though we once regarded Christ according to the flesh, we regard him thus no longer. [17] Therefore, if anyone is in Christ, he is a new creation. The old has passed away; behold, the new has come. [18] All this is from God, who through Christ reconciled us to himself and gave us the ministry of reconciliation; [19] that is, in Christ God was reconciling the world to himself, not counting their trespasses against them, and entrusting to us the message of reconciliation. [20] Therefore, we are ambassadors for Christ, God making his appeal through us. We implore you on behalf of Christ, be

reconciled to God. ²¹ For our sake he made him to be sin who knew no sin, so that in him we might become the righteousness of God.

⁶:¹ Working together with him, then, we appeal to you not to receive the grace of God in vain. ² For he says, "In a favorable time I listened to you, and in a day of salvation I have helped you."

Behold, now is the favorable time; behold, now is the day of salvation. ³ We put no obstacle in anyone's way, so that no fault may be found with our ministry, ⁴ but as servants of God we commend ourselves in every way: by great endurance, in afflictions, hardships, calamities, ⁵ beatings, imprisonments, riots, labors, sleepless nights, hunger; ⁶ by purity, knowledge, patience, kindness, the Holy Spirit, genuine love; ⁷ by truthful speech, and the power of God; with the weapons of righteousness for the right hand and for the left; ⁸ through honor and dishonor, through slander and praise. We are treated as impostors, and yet are true; ⁹ as unknown, and yet well known; as dying, and behold, we live; as punished, and yet not killed; ¹⁰ as sorrowful, yet always rejoicing; as poor, yet making many rich; as having nothing, yet possessing everything.

Recap *Jesus died, so that we might not live for ourselves, but live for Him. If we are in Christ, we are a new creation. The old identity is gone and we have a new identity in Christ. Jesus restored our relationship with God, and so that is now our message: to call people to be restored to God. Jesus was made sin for us, so that we might be the righteousness of God—His love on earth. The appeal is not to receive God's grace in vain, because now is the day of salvation. Jesus' followers go through all kinds of sufferings. Though physically poor, they are spiritually rich, and though in the eyes of the world they have nothing, in reality they possess everything in God.*

Q: Do we want to be made into a new creation?
- *Get feedback.*

Q: When is the day of salvation?
- *Now. Right now. Today is the day of salvation.*

> Jesus is offering each one of you the gift of His love and presence and eternal life. Please don't receive the grace of God in vain. Today is the day of your salvation. He has designed you. He has called you by name. He has chosen you. What is your response? If you haven't already, will you give your life to Jesus? Will you follow Him?

Leaders
- Let people respond honestly. Some people may decide the cost of following Jesus is too high. That's fine. Still encourage these people to pray and express their heart honestly to God.
- It may be that some people in the group are not quite ready to decide to follow Jesus, but don't want to decide against Him either. That's fine. Just ask them if they would like God to help them to become ready. If so, encourage them to pray and ask God for His help.
- If people want to follow Jesus then have each person pray in turn and commit their lives to Jesus. Let them express it in their own words. Don't worry if they don't tick all the boxes of the "sinner's prayer". Let them just say what's on their heart and freely express their decision to follow God in their own words.

When people make a commitment to follow Jesus, take some time to celebrate. Even think about organizing a more formal celebration. This is the most important day in their lives—enjoy it and give everyone else a chance to celebrate it.

Where to from Here?

Leaders
If you have a number of people who have committed their lives to Jesus then ask if they would like to continue meeting to keep learning and growing together. If you'd like to continue studying together, please feel free to visit www.discoverjesus.today for further discipleship resources.

Q: Who would like to continue meeting together?

12 | Home Reading and Questions

☐ **Hebrews 10:12-17**
Q: How great was Jesus' sacrifice to conquer sin?

Q: Can any sin remain after being washed by the blood of Jesus?

Q: If the Law of God is love, what would it be like to have God's law written on my heart and mind?

☐ **2 Timothy 3:10-17**
Q: What does God promise in this passage?

Q: Why must persecutions come to people who just want to live a godly life in Christ?

Q: What does it mean for me to continue on in the things I have become convinced of?

☐ **Ephesians 1:15-22**
Q: What would it be like to receive a spirit of wisdom and revelation in the knowledge of Jesus?

Q: What is the hope of my calling?

Q: What are the riches of glory of my inheritance in Jesus?

Q: What would it be like for me to experience the surpassing power of Jesus?

Q: Is there anything that can stand against God's power in Jesus?

☐ **Prayer** *Write your own prayer to Jesus here:*

☐ **Acts 6-7**

Write down your questions here:

☐ Experiences with God
Write down some of your own prayers, discoveries, questions and experiences.

discoverjesus.today

www.ingramcontent.com/pod-product-compliance
Lightning Source LLC
LaVergne TN
LVHW061216060426
835507LV00016B/1957